OCT - 4 1994 DATE DUE

DISCARD

973.04
S

COPY 81

Smit, Pamela, comp.
    The Dutch in America, 1609-1970; a
chronology & fact book. Compiled and
edited by Pamela and J. W. Smit. Dobbs
Ferry, N.Y., Oceana Publications, 1972.
    vi, 116 p. 23 cm. (onology
series, no. 5)

    SUMMARY: A   utch in
America from   erti-
nent documen
    ISBN 0-379-

    1. Dutch America   ory.

31502   My78

72-8684
MARC AC

ETHNIC CHRONOLOGY SERIES
NUMBER 5

The Dutch in America
1609-1970
A Chronology & Fact Book

Compiled and edited by
Pamela and J.W. Smit

1972
OCEANA PUBLICATIONS, INC.
DOBBS FERRY, NEW YORK

Library of Congress Cataloging in Publication Data

Smit, Jacobus Wilhelmus, comp.
　The Dutch in America, 1609-1970.

　(Ethnic chronology series, no. 5)
　SUMMARY: A chronology of the Dutch in America
from 1609 to 1970 with pertinent documents included.
　Bibliography: p.
　1. Dutch in the United States--History.
[1. Dutch in the United States--History]　I. Title.
II. Series.
E184.D9S6　　　973'.04'3931　　　72-8684
ISBN 0-379-00504-2

©Copyright 1972 by Oceana Publications, Inc.

All rights reserved. No part of this publication may be reproduced or
transmitted in any form or by any means, electronic or mechanical, including photocopy, recording, xerography, or any information storage
and retrieval system, without permission in writing from the publisher.

Manufactured in the United States of America

TABLE OF CONTENTS

INTRODUCTION

In undertaking a survey of the Dutch involvement in America one is immediately confronted by two chronologically separate but not totally independent phenomena: Dutch sovereignity over part of the American northeast in the seventeenth century, and the wave of Dutch immigration in the second half of the nineteenth century. While the rulers of New Netherland left only a small population behind to carry on the traditions of Holland in America, many of these colonial Dutch survived to form a non-English Establishment in New York. Today the colonial Dutch presence along the Hudson River is preserved by the Dutch place-names and by the Church left behind by the defeated New Netherlanders. The Reformed Church in America, the direct descendant of the colonial Dutch church, represents the great link between the two groups of American Dutch.

The importance of the Reformed Church in the relationship between the "Old" and "New" Dutch, and, indeed, in the latter group's Americanization, cannot be overemphasized. The Hudson River Valley Dutch had clung stubbornly to their religion, and as they grew rich, so did their Church. By the time the "New Immigration" began in 1846, the Reformed Church in America had all the trappings of an old established church: colleges, theological seminaries, large, well-organized congregations, and considerable capital. Van Raalte's decision to merge his Secessionist congregations with the Reformed Church in America - and the Reformed hierarchy's decision to accept them - accounts to a large extent for the swift tempo of Americanization among the later Dutch arrivals as well as for this group's lack of a feeling of alienation from American society in general, an estrangement tragically felt by many other immigrant groups. The Dutch predate the Pilgrims in America; their awareness of this is unquestionably a source of the sense of security the later Dutch exhibited about their right to a role as American citizens. The rest of the nation's awareness of the historical role of the Dutch was another factor in this easy adjustment: every school child knows of Peter Stuyvesant; there was no need for Dutch fraternal societies to search the pages of American history for obscure Revolutionary heroes in order to remind people that the Dutch had played a part in the building of America.

In making up this chronology of events and people important to the Dutch experience in America, our criterion for inclusion of outstanding individuals has not been whether they had Dutch names but whether they were conscious of their Netherlands descent. It would be a useless exercise to include all the prominent people in American history who had Dutch surnames; one's name is inherited from one's father but does not necessarily determine one's cultural affinity. In some cases we have also included people who, although not of Dutch descent, played significant roles in the Dutch community.

It must be remembered that in speaking of Dutch immigration we are dealing with a small group in the context of total immigration to this country. There were 10,000 people in New Netherland at the time of the British take-over, of which many were English, French, or German; the figures for the later immigration, available from 1820 to the present, include no more than 270,000. Compared to the four and a quarter million Irish or 5,300,000 Germans who came to this country between 1820 and 1920, the Dutch represented the merest trickle, less, in fact, than the Slovaks or the Greeks. Yet the Dutch have played a role in the United States that is significant out of all proportion to their small numbers. This may be explained partially by the fact that the city which they founded and came to dominate became the most prominent in America, carrying them to prominence with it. This tiny group of New York Dutch gave the republic three presidents in its first 175 years of independence, being the only non-British group in America to send a man to the White House during that time.

There has always been some confusion in the American mind between the German and Dutch national groups. Until recently the word "Dutch" was widely used to refer to the Germans, the "Deutsch". There is a certain logic to this confusion, since the linguistic border between Germany and the Netherlands is very ill-defined, with the Germans in the vicinity of the Dutch border speaking a Low German dialect very similar to Dutch. (Politically, however, the two cultures could not be more separate; the Netherlands has enjoyed a republican form of government since the sixteenth century, while the German states knew only absolutism until after World War I.) In several cases we have included individuals or groups from the German areas near the border which were linguistically and culturally part of the Greater Netherlands; religiously this area of Germany was totally dominated by the Calvinistic Reformed Church of the Netherlands, to which the border Germans looked for their ministers and for their order of worship.

There are, of course, still Hollanders coming to America, although since the Immigration Act of 1924, Dutch interest has shifted radically to Canada and Australia; at the present moment, moreover, with prosperity in the Netherlands at an all-time high, Dutch emigration has ceased to be very significant. Those few still arriving in the United States no longer gravitate to the traditional settlements in Michigan, Iowa and New Jersey, but stay in the cities, where their continued ethnic consciousness is attested to by the recent establishment of many Dutch social and sports clubs in the California and New York areas. To what extent their lot is affected by the centuries of Dutch history in America can only be speculated; one may assume, however, that if these recent arrivals have any contact at all with the earlier Dutch-American traditions, it is through the Reformed Churches, which remain strong and influential. Thus it is not irrelevant to the modern Dutch-American experience that we have given so much space in this chronology to the developments and schisms in the Church, for with the colonial Dutch, and to an even greater extent with the nineteenth century immigrants, their history is the history of the Reformed Church in America.

CHRONOLOGY

I. The Original Wave of Dutch Immigration

    A. The First Immigrants

1609   Henry Hudson, English navigator, hired by Dutch East India Company to explore possible route to India via the Arctic Ocean, north of Russia. Failing to do this, Hudson headed west in his ship, the Half Moon, investigated the East Coast of North America and headed his ship up the present-day Hudson River as far as the site of Albany.

1610   First Dutch trading ship sails to mouth of Hudson River.

1614   Dutch explorer Adriaan Block charted the coast of New York and Long Island, investigating also the mouths of the Housatonic and Connecticut Rivers.

                  Founding of the short-lived Fort Nassau, near the site of Albany, as a fur-trading center.

1621   States General of the United Provinces of the Netherlands formed the Dutch West India Company. All the lands between the Delaware (South) River and Cape Cod were claimed on the basis of Hudson's voyage. The company was to exercise a total monopoly on all the commercial activity within its realms. The fur trade, not colonization, was to be its main focus, a fact symbolized by the beaver in the coat of arms and seal of the Province of New Netherland.

1624   Peter Minuit was named the first Director-general of the Dutch West India Company, which he remained until replaced in 1633 by Wouter van Twiller.

                  March 31. Departure from Holland of the ship "Nieuw Nederland", carrying 30 Walloon families to be settled by the West India Company on its lands, first at Fort Orange (now Albany), the first permanent Dutch settlement in America, then at Fort Good Hope on the Connecticut River (1633), and at Fort Nassau on the Delaware (South) River. The realms of the company were to be known as New Netherland, and the first governor of the province was Willem Verhulst.

Incorporation of the Reformed Church in New York and New Jersey. Calvinism had been the state religion of the Netherlands since the Reformation and became so firmly established on American soil under Dutch rule that it survived the take-over by the British in 1664.

1625   The beginning of the construction of Fort Amsterdam on Manhattan Island, designed by engineer Cryn Fredericksz, to serve as a naval base.

In an effort to make the colony agriculturally productive enough to victual the trading ships of the West India Company, as well as to feed itself, the company introduced a system of farms or boweries (from Dutch bouwerij, "farm") worked on shares. The company supplied the boweries with livestock and equipment but they failed to flourish, and by 1652 all of the company boweries were sold. During this period, however, the Dutch introduced the culture of beets, edives, spinach, dill, parsley and chervil.

1626   Peter Minuit brings the previously widely-dispersed settlers together on Manhattan Island. By 1628 New Amsterdam had a population of 270.

1628   Jonas Michaelius organized the first Reformed congregation in New Netherland at New Amsterdam.

1629   The company extends wide-ranging privileges to certain entrepreneurs, or patroons, in exchange for their founding agricultural settlements of at least 50 people. The grants were to extend either four leagues along both sides of such a river, and as far inland as the patroon saw fit, except that Manhattan Island was to be reserved for the company. The company gave the patroons hereditary rights to their land, including the rights to fish, fowl and grind, as well as civil and criminal jurisdiction over their settlers. The patroons were in return expected to provide schooling for the children of the settlers. The first patroonships to be established were those of Kilaen van Rensselaer at Rensselaerswyck, near Albany, and Michael Pauw's Pavonia, opposite Fort Amsterdam on the mainland. Except for that of Van Rensselaer, all the patroonships were sold back to the company in the following years, owing largely to the company's hostile and jealous attitude towards its own entrepreneurs. Rensselaerswyck, however, flourished.

An interesting footnote to the West India Co.'s directive
to the patroons was its advice concerning relations with
the Indians. Clause 26 of the directive stated that "Whosoever shall settle any colony out of the limits of Manhattan Island shall be obliged to satisfy the Indians for the land
they shall settle upon". It is worthwhile to compare this
to the Massachusetts statute of 1633 which confirmed to
the Indians the little patches of land around their wigwams
but declared the rest the property of the whites on the authority of Chapter I, Genesis, "and the invitation of the
Indians".

1631-
1664

Foundation of many communities in New Netherland, including Swanendael (now Lewes, Del.) in 1631 (it was destroyed by Indians in 1632); Beverwyck (1634) near Albany; Gravezande (Gravesend, N. Y.) in 1642; Heemstede
(Hempstead, N. Y.) in 1644; Vliessingen (now Flushing,
N. Y.) in 1645; Yonkers in 1646; Breuckelen (now Brooklyn, N. Y.) in 1646; Vlack Bos (now Flatbush, N. Y.) in
1652; New Utrecht in 1657; New Haarlem (now Harlem,
N. Y.) in 1658; and Wiltwyck (now Kingston, N. Y.) in 1661.
Most of the settlers engaged in agricultural work were from
the Netherlands provinces of Utrecht and Gelderland; the
prosperity of the Netherlands in the seventeenth century
was restricted to the western and coastal regions, while
the eastern agricultural areas remained poor, their econ-
omies hard hit by the Eighty Years War with Spain.

1638

Large number of Dutch were to be found at Fort Christina,
a Swedish Colony on the Delaware River which had been
founded in the mid 1630's by 22 Dutch settlers brought over
by Peter Minuit, formerly Director-general of the Dutch
West India Company, but now a member of the New Sweden
Company. The only Swede in the settlement was the commander of the fort. In 1640 another boatful of Dutch (from
Utrecht) joined the community.

1639

Arrival in New Netherland of entire English communities
from Puritan New England, who, in their search for religious freedom, chose to settle on Long Island under the
Dutch flag rather than stay in Massachusetts and be per-
secuted for their non-conformity.

Encroachments by the British along the Dutch-held Connecticut River, where they attacked Fort Good Hope,
claiming that the Dutch, by failing to cultivate the land in
Connecticut, had lost any legal claim to it which they might
have had.

1640   As a result of a decline in immigration, and under the prod-
            ding of the States General, the Dutch West India Company
            adopted a more liberal policy towards trade and immigra-
            tion. The company's monopoly of the fur trade with the
            Indians was terminated, and patroonships were made easier
            to acquire. For a short time, free passage was available
            from the Netherlands to anyone willing to settle in New
            Netherland. The immigration policy was a success and
            many people, including English, French (Huguenots), Ger-
            mans, Norwegians and Swedes, the latter famous for their
            skill as loggers, settled on company land.

1640-   Willem Kieft, Director-general of the West India Company
1645   1637-1646, mistakenly began the First Indian War, a blood-
            bath which had a catastrophic effect on the colony. The
            population of New Netherland declined sharply from about
            3,000 to 1,000. Kieft was fired and replaced in 1646 by
            Peter Stuyvesant, the former governor of Dutch Curacao.

1642   Reformed congregations established at Rensselaerswyck
            and Fort Orange by Johannes Megapolensis, the most effec-
            tive of the early Reformed ministers. Megapolensis
            learned the tongue of the Mohawk Indians, whom he evan-
            gelized, and subsequently wrote a treatise about them
            which was widely read in the Netherlands.

1651   Jan Baptist van Rensselaer comes from the Netherlands
            to supervise the patroonship founded by his father at
            Rensselaerswyck. Kiliaen, the founder, never visited
            America, but supervised his holdings from the Nether-
            lands; thus Jan Baptist was the first in America of a fam-
            ily that was to exercise virtually feudal power in upper
            New York State until the middle of the 19th century.

            Director-general Stuyvesant built Fort Casimir on the
            Delaware River to challenge the Swedish at Fort Christina.

1652   New Amsterdam was granted self-government and the priv-
            ileges of free trade were widened. The new freedoms were
            a result of an appeal to the States General of the Nether-
            lands by an embassy under Adriaen van der Donck, who pro-
            tested the oppressiveness of the West India Company.

1654   Swedes take over Fort Casimir on the Delaware and natu-
            ralize its settlers.

            Seventy orphan boys and girls are sent from Amsterdam to
            New Netherland as apprentice workers and future colonists.

1655   Appearance in Amsterdam of Jonkheer Adriaen van der
        Donck's Description of New Netherland, which was influ-
        ential in stirring up interest about America. He stressed
        the fruitfulness of the land and the essential friendliness
        of the Indians, who, according to van der Donck, were
        alienated by the perfidy of the white man. Van der Donck
        himself had settled on a grant of land above New Amster-
        dam which is the present-day site of Yonkers, N. Y. The
        name Yonkers is a corruption of Van der Donck's title of
        Jonkheer.

        The city of Amsterdam, interested in relocating its indi-
        gent and refugee population to a colony in the New World,
        as well as in developing its own source of naval stores,
        buys a patroonship on the Delaware River, on land which
        Stuyvesant had just conquered from Sweden. The city
        published extensive propaganda for its settlement at "New
        Amstel", as the patroonship was called. The first boat-
        load of colonists arrived in April, 1657, and settled on the
        site of the present Newcastle. By 1659 there were 600
        colonists at New Amstel, but the settlement was wiped out
        in 1664; unlike New Amsterdam, New Amstel resisted the
        British attack and was consequently plundered (against
        British orders), and its soldiers were taken as laborers
        to Virginia.

        Second Indian War again brought great destruction and
        slaughter to New Netherland, largely due to the settlers'
        stubborn refusal to spend the money necessary for the
        construction of defenses around their villages.

        September 25. Peter Stuyvesant secured the bloodless
        surrender of Fort Christina and all of New Sweden to the
        Dutch.

1660   The first Reformed congregation in present-day New Jer-
        sey was founded in Bergen (now Jersey City). Many more
        Dutch were to move to New Jersey from New York during
        the brief period when the British Governor of New York,
        Cornbury (1702-1708) made difficulties for the Dutch Re-
        formed Churches in his province. These later immigrants
        settled in the Raritan and Millstone Valleys.

1661   Arend van Curler founded the city of Schenectady.

        Peter Cornelisz. Plockhoy began publishing pamphlets
        containing his plans for a christian communist colony on
        the Delaware River. He contracted with the West India

Company for land which was to be held jointly by all the future settlers.

1662

Plockhoy settled near Swanendael with 25 Mennonite families, who shared his faith in a communal way of life. Plockhoy was thus the first man to use the New World as a laboratory for a social experiment, as it would so often be used later. Plockhoy and his followers represent, moreover, the only example of spontaneous group migration in the history of New Netherland. The little colony was wiped out by the British in 1664 and many of its settlers were transported to Virginia as laborers and servants.

1664

The fall of New Netherland to the British. On the eve of the British take-over the population of New Netherland was about 10,000, having soared from 2,000 in 1646. The 10,000 consisted primarily of Dutch, but included also English, French, Huguenots, Walloons, and Germans. New Amsterdam's population was about 1500. The colony was just emerging as an important grain exporter to the Netherlands.

1673

Reconquest of New York by the Dutch, who christened New York City New Orange and Albany Willemstad.

1674

Treaty of Westminster, whereby the Dutch returned its North American possessions to England.

1683

Over 100 Dutch Labadists from the province of Friesland settle on three thousand acres near Augustine, Maryland. As followers of Jean de Labadie, they held it essential for man to withdraw from the world in order to lead a life of perfect piety. Like the Quakers, the Labadistes stressed the importance of the inner light and a strict ethical code. Their church was only for the elect, and strict communism was practiced by the community. By 1730 the colony had died out.

Settlement near Germantown, Pa. of group of Dutch Mennonites, who had been living in Krefeld and Kriesheim in Germany. The Mennonites bought 5,000 acres from William Penn, who was half Dutch himself and who had been encouraging immigration to his colony by Netherlanders by publishing pamphlets in Dutch. Soon this original group was joined by other Dutch Mennonites from Goch and Mülheim on the Ruhr, and in 1685 by the wealthy Amsterdam merchant Jacob Telner, who became the largest landowner in Germantown. Until 1709 Germantown remained essentially a Dutch community, but the sheer weight of numbers of the German immigrants to Pennsylvania in the early 18th century soon erased most traces of the early Dutch settlement.

1684   Pennsylvania authorities began to look more and more to Germany for colonists, as conditions there were more impoverished than in the Netherlands in the Golden Age. Pastorius, the father of German immigration to Pennsylvania, wrote his parents to "send only Germans"..."the Hollanders, (as sad experience has taught me) are not so easily satisfied, which in this new land is a very necessary quality".

1688   February 18. A group of Quakers in Germantown, Pa., among whom the Dutch were prominent, made the first formal protest against slavery in the western hemisphere.

B. The Legacy of the Original Dutch Settlers

1. Under British Rule (1674-1775)

1683   First meeting of the New York provincial parliament sanctioned by James II. 60% of its members were Dutch. Even after the English take-over, the Dutch remained culturally, socially and in many ways politically the most influential element. Most of the most powerful and rich members of the Dutch community stayed on, including Peter Stuyvesant and the Van Rensselaers. Additional strength was given their group by the fact that after the revocation of the Edict of Nantes in France in 1685, thousands of Huguenots sought refuge in Holland, whose Calvinism was sympathetic to them; many of these Huguenots, totally Netherlandicized, immigrated subsequently to America, where they worshipped in Dutch Reformed Churches and were members of the Dutch community.

1688   "The Glorious Revolution" in England, when William of Orange and his Protestants took over the throne from King James II, a Catholic sympathizer. One indication of the political conservatism of the established Dutch citizens in New York was their loyalty to the local officials appointed by James, whose favors had frequently been assured by large bribes. In the confusion that resulted, a demogogic populist, Leisler, took over New York for the common people in the name of William. The Dutch aristocracy, fearful for the status quo in which they were prospering, refused to recognize Leisler in spite of the fact that he was a member of the Dutch community and was seizing power in the name of William of Orange, a Protestant Dutch ruler. Some of the Dutch patriciate were imprisoned by Leisler. So great was their influence with the British, however, that once William's authority was confirmed in England, the wealthy Dutch of New York arranged for Leisler to be condemned to death as a revolutionary. This sentence was backed enthusiastically by the officials of the Dutch Reformed Church, who were themselves large landowners.

1695   Publication of the report of Rev. J. Miller on the New York colony. - According to the report, the colony contained 3,525 church-going families, of which 1,754 were Dutch. In the city of New York were 800 families, of which 500 were Dutch. Modern historians estimate the total number of Dutch living in America in 1700 at around 8,650, with 6,650 in New York, 1,000 in New Jersey, and 1,000 in Delaware and Pennsylvania. Rev. Miller goes on in his report to classify the Dutch community as wealthy, while the English and French groups were, respectively, in moderate circumstances and poor. An example of the prosperity of the Dutch in New York was Cornelis Steenwyck, a wine dealer and the richest man in the province, who left a fortune of 53,000 guilders at his death in 1686. The Roosevelts and Van Cortlandts remained the biggest sugar refiners, and the Cuylers and Rhinelanders ran the big rum distilleries. Under British rule the Dutch landed gentry also grew in power, and families like the De Schuylers, Van Dams, Beekmans, Van Brughs and Cortlandts exercised the feudal privileges of hunting rights, baking rights and milling rights. (These lordly rights were relinquished at the time of the American Revolution, but in some cases, notably that of the Van Rensselaers, some feudal privileges were practised far into the 19th century.)

1703   Death and famous funeral of Pieter Jacob Marius, official of the Dutch Reformed Church and the richest man in New York City. It was said that every man on Manhattan Island owed Marius money; at his funeral 29 gallons of wine and 800 cakes were consumed.

1700–   "Great Awakening" in Dutch Reformed congregations in
1792   the area of the former New Netherlands between the Hudson and Delaware Rivers. In 1708 there were only 34 Reformed congregations in America, by 1750 there were 65. These congregations were served chiefly by Dutch ministers, accounting for a small but influential immigration of Dutch intellectuals throughout the 18th century.

One of the most distinguished of these was Theodore J. Frelinghuysen (1691-1748), a native of Lingen, Germany, but steeped in the traditions of Dutch Calvinism. He preached in Raritan, N. J., and was a strong advocate of church autonomy as opposed to dependence on the church authorities in the Netherlands.

1737   Publication of the "Fundamental Articles for the Ecclesiastical Coetus (Assembly) of the Classis of Amsterdam". This was an attempt by an autonomy-minded group of Reformed ministers in America to wrest some authority for the direction of American Reformed congregations from the classis of Amsterdam. Another group of Reformed ministers, the Conferentie, opposed them, advocating continued dependence on the Dutch church.

1763   Appointment in New York City of a Scot, Dr. Archibald Laidlie, as first bilingual minister in a Dutch Reformed church in America. This appointment was indicative of the gradual "Americanization" of the church and of the Dutch community as a whole. The last Reformed minister to get his theological education in the Netherlands was another Scot, Dr. John Henry Livingston, founder of the famous Hudson River dynasty of that name, who was educated at Utrecht before coming to preach in America.

1771   Schism in the Reformed Church ended between the Coetus group, signers of the "Fundamental Articles" who sought autonomy for the American church, and the Conferentie group, who opposed independence.

1772   The classis of the Amsterdam Dutch Reformed Church concedes greater independence of action to the American church.

  2. Revolutionary Period and After

1775-   The American Revolution. The Dutch community in New
1783   York was outraged by the passing of the Stamp Act, and many Dutch families, among them the Roosevelts and the Rutgers, came out publicly against it. Ministers of the Dutch Reformed Church were so vehemently pro-rebel that British officers permitted their troops to plunder Dutch churches. Many Dutch families, such as the Schuylers, Frelinghuysens, Rutgers and Cortlandts, were active on

the rebel side, to the extent that Washington reckoned the
Dutch as among his best soldiers and referred to the New
Jersey-Hudson region as his "loyal Dutch belt". The
rebel forces depended largely on Dutch merchants to supply
their war materials. At the beginning of the war, this trade
centered around the Dutch island of St. Eustatius in the
Carribean, but as early as 1776 there was regular inter-
course between the rebellious colonies and the Netherlands
ports. The opening of the Revolution had, of course, marked the end of the authority of the English Navigation Acts,
which had restricted colonial trade with powers other
than Britain. These acts were officially repudiated by
Congress on April 6, 1776, at which point formal trade with
the Netherlands could begin.

1782   John Adams travelled to Holland to stimulate interest in
trade and investment in the United States. He returned to
America with a 5 million guilder loan for Congress.

September 17. Formal treaty of trade and friendship made
between the republics of the Netherlands and the United
States.

1790's   Population pressure in New Jersey and Pennsylvania causes
a large group of Dutch families to make the trek west to
"the cane lands of Kaintuckee". Many settled in Mercer
County, Kentucky, at the mouth of the Salt River, where
there was a Dutch Reformed congregation as early as
1800. The New York, or "Mohawk" Dutch, went chiefly to
Michigan, whose capital, Lansing, bears the name of an
old Albany Dutch family. These established Michigan
Dutch were to be of inestimable service to the wave of new
Dutch settlers in Michigan in the mid 19th century.

1792   Complete independence of the Reformed Church in America
from the classis in Amsterdam. It was known successively
as the "Reformed Dutch Church of North America", "Dutch
and English were used side by side. In that year, around
250,000 communicants still attended completely Dutch services, but as early as 1803 the last Dutch sermon was
preached in New York City, where the process of Americanization had been accelerated by the pressures of urban
life. But by 1820 English was the general language of the
Reformed Church, even among the more isolated congregations of the Mohawk Dutch. At the time at which it became
independent from Amsterdam, the American church had 116
congregations. By 1845, on the eve of the next great wave
of Dutch immigration, there were 274 congregations in
America. Great expansion had taken place in spite of the

fact that in 1822 a number of congregations under the leadership of Dr. S. Froeligh of Hackensack, N. J., had separated from the main church in protest againsts its progressiveness and Americanization. Their group was known as the "True Dutch Reformed Church" (not to be confused with the Seceders of 1857 who took the same name).

1794

Cornelius Vanderbilt (van der Bilt) was born on Staten Island, the son of a ferryman. After amassing a fortune in railroads he died in 1877 personally worth 105 million dollars; the family of which he was the founder was worth 700 million dollars at that time. Many other descendants of the original Dutch settlers, some of whose families had been poor or of only moderate wealth, made huge fortunes in the post Civil War land boom. These included the Schermerhorns, the Roosevelts and the Rutgers.

1800-
1840

Growth of interest among Dutch descendants about their ancestry and Holland. A great stimulus to this interest had been the publication in 1809 of Washington Irving's enormously popular A History of New York, a comic chronicle alledgedly written by one Diedrich Knickerbocker (hence the term "Knickerbocker Dutch" for New York Dutch). Hermanus Bleecker, a member of an old New Amsterdam family, was appointed minister to Holland, and the Van Rensselaers and Duyckinks visited the Netherlands for sentimental reasons. J. Romeyn Brodhead, also of Dutch descent, went to Holland as a member of the American legation, and while he was there collected material for his famous Colonial History of the State of New York. Dutch was still cultivated in some of the very highest social circles of America, as was attested to by a letter from the Dutch exile Van der Kemp to his children, saying that his wife had spoken Dutch with Mrs. Clinton and Mrs. Hamilton, wives of the Governor of New York and the Secretary of the Treasury. At the other end of the social ladder Dutch also proved durable: Until 1880 "Bergen County Dutch" was the common idiom of rural northern New Jersey.

1820

Founding of the St. Nicholas Society in Albany, followed by the founding of a New York chapter in 1835. Both branches celebrated with an annual feast on St. Nicholas Day, December 5; the Albany chapter's emphasis was benevolent, providing aid to the needy of Dutch descent; the downstate branch concentrated on the historical aspects of early Dutch settlement in New York.

1837 -
1841

Martin Van Buren, of Kinderhook, N. Y., served as President of the United States. There have been too many descendants of 17th century Dutch settlers in politics to ennumerate them separately; besides three presidents, there have been several vice-presidents and numerous congressmen. The first governor of New York, De Witt Clinton, was of Dutch ancestry, as was Van Wyck, the first mayor of Greater New York.

1855

The opening of Castle Garden as a compulsory landing place for all immigrants was due largely to the efforts of Dutch-descended Gulian C. Verplanck, Commissioner of Emigration. Up until this time, immigrants were robbed, cheated and horribly exploited by unscrupulous hotel and railway agents when they disembarked at New York, not infrequently losing their life's savings within a few hours. But only certified officials were allowed entry to Castle Garden, where immigrants were given sound information, the official currency exchange rate, and were sold railroad tickets at a fair price. The Commissioner of Emigration was subject to much criticism for his interference of the state in the "private enterprise" of immigrant exploitation; of all the legacies of the New Amsterdam Dutch to the 19th century Dutch immigrants, however, none was to be so practically beneficial as Verplanck's work.

1885

Holland Society founded in New York City. Its membership was restricted to descendants "in the direct male line of a Dutchman who was a native or resident of New York or of the American colonies prior to the year 1675". In 1888 members of the Society made a pilgrimage to the Netherlands, and in 1889 it sent a telegram of greetings to the Boers of South Africa referring to their common descent from 17th century Dutch immigrants. The Society is still active in New York City.

1905-
1909

Theodore Roosevelt, member of old New York Dutch family, served as President of the United States. Very conscious of his Dutch heritage, Roosevelt was able to quote Dutch sayings and verses from his childhood during his visit to the Netherlands.

1933-
1945

Franklin Delano Roosevelt served as President of the United States, dying just months before the troops of which he was Commander in Chief liberated the Netherlands from the German occupation. His wife Eleanor, niece of Theodore, was more steeped in the "Knickerbocker" tradition than he, and could recall that the very elderly members of her family still spoke Dutch on Sundays.

II. Dutch Immigration to the United States of America

    A. Individual Immigration

When, after the short-lived bid for power of the Dutch "Patriots", or democrats, was ended by the restoration of the Oranges in 1787, many of the deposed party emigrated to America, as a country sympathetic to their ideals. The confusion of the Napoleonic wars led to more emigration, which in turn attracted the attention of some Dutch Catholics, who were severely restricted in their activities in the Netherlands. Financial interests were also attracted by the possibility of investment.

1783   Andre Everard van Braam Houckgeest (1739-1801) of Zutphen was appointed Dutch consul to America. In 1784, when the Patriots were attempting their take-over, he became an American citizen. In 1794-95 he visited the Imperial Chinese court, after which he built the famous "Chinese Retreat" on the Delaware, filling it with his priceless collection of Chinese art. A friend of Washington, Lafayette and Talleyrand, he travelled in the highest circles of American society. He did in Holland in 1801.

1788   May 4. Arrival in New York of Francois Adriaan van der Kemp (born 1752), a Mennonite minister and former member of the Dutch Patriots Party. He had been jailed in Holland for his advocacy of the overthrow of ancient and unjust practices and his rationalist political and religious beliefs. Regarding the United States as the land of the future, he brought his family with him and settled at Oldenbarneveld, N. Y., where he was the leader of a small Dutch cultural colony. He was a friend of Lafayette and Adams as well as many of America's literati of the time. His articles on historical subjects were highly regarded in intellectual circles, and he was commissioned by New York's Governor De Witt Clinton, who called him "the most learned man in America" to translate the colonial records of New York. Harvard College awarded him an honorary Doctor of Laws degree. He died September 7, 1829.

1788   Arrival of Father Theodorus Brouwers, a Rotterdamer, in Philadelphia. He bought large tracts of land in Westmoreland County, which was to be the site of St. Vincent's Arch Abbey of the Benedictine Order, and was the first Catholic priest to establish himself in Western Pennsylvania.

1796   February 13. Establishment of Holland Land Company in Amsterdam by prominent members of the Dutch Patriots Party. Large tracts of land in northwest Pennsylvania, along the Niagra River in New York State, as well as interests in the maple sugar industry, were bought up by Patriot bankers Nicolas and Jacob van Staphorst and P. and C. van Eeghen, who formed the Company with Patriot attorney and politician Rutger Jan Schimmelpenninck, along with the firms of Pieter Stadnitski and Son, Ten Cate and Vollenhoven and Willem and J. Willink. 896 shares were offered for sale on the Amsterdam market. Not all of the Company's projects were successful, but it was implemental in the development of the Genesee region of New York State, where the Company cooperated in the construction of the Erie Canal, which was finished in 1825. In 1803 the Company had chosen the mouth of Buffalo Creek for the site of its village of New Amsterdam, whose name was later changed to Buffalo, N. Y.

1805   Father Charles Nerenckx, born at Herffelingen, Brabant, arrived in Kentucky. Here he founded the Society of the Sisters of Loretto at the Foot of the Cross and began the flow to America of a group of Netherlands priests, including the Flemings Pieter De Smet (born in Dendermonde in 1801, died 1873), active in the northwest, and the Dutch brothers Adriaan and Christiaan Hoecken, missionaries among the Blackfoot and Kickapoo Indians. The same group is responsible for founding the Jesuit house at Florissant, near St. Louis.

1810   Arrival in Philadelphia from Holland of Dr. Gerard Troost (1776-1850), medical doctor, pharmacist and formerly geologist to King Louis Napoleon of Holland. In 1812 he helped found the Philadelphia Academy of Natural Sciences and was its president until 1817. Later he was associated with Robert Owen's utopian society at New Harmony, Indiana. Troost was eventually named geologist and minerologist to the State of Tennessee.

B. "The New Immigration"

    1. Economic Depression in the Netherlands.

1815   The whole period was one of depressed economic condi-
1860   tions in Holland. Dutch manufacturing was left far behind by the industrial revolution in England and Belgium. Hamburg and London began to overshadow Amsterdam as trading centers and the expense of resisting the Belgian

revolt led to the levying of oppressively high taxes. The failure of the potato crops of 1845 and 1846 led to widespread hunger among the agricultural workers, who were to make up the bulk of immigrants to America.

2. The Church Reform of 1816

1816

In 1815 King William I of Orange-Nassau had become King of Holland (including Belgium until 1830). He was the moving spirit behind the reorganization of the Reformed Church in the Netherlands in 1816 which granted the crown wider executive powers and which introduced a new doctrine to which ministers had to subscribe: Formerly they were obliged to accept the Belgic Confession, the Heidelberg Catechism and the Canons of Dordrecht "because (quia) they agree with God's word." Now they were forced to accept these doctrines "in so far as (quatenus) they are in harmony with God's word contained in doctrinal standards". The controversy which arose around the two doctrines of quia and quatenus was responsible for the Secession of 1834.

1828

Publication of Izaac Da Costa's Scruples Against the Spirit of the Age, a protest against the type of rationalist religious philosophy that was responsible for the Reform of 1816. Da Costa was a leader of the Dutch Réveil, the intellectual movement encouraging a return to the strict beliefs of the early Reformed Church; the Réveil had great influence on the leaders of the Secession of 1834.

1834

October 14. "Act of Secession and Return" published by Hendrik De Cock of Ulrum, who, like the leaders of the Réveil, felt that seventeenth century pietism (as represented by the theologians Voetius and Van Lodenstein) was preferable to the rationalism of modern Reformed teaching. Particularly objectionable to the seceders were the Evangelische Gezangen, a collection of hymns used to supplement the psalms in the modern churches. The dissenters were to describe these hymns as "192 siren songs, designed to draw the members of the Reformed Church from their Savior and to carry them into the false doctrine of lies." De Cock was suspended from the main body of the Church, as were his followers Hendrik P. Scholte, Antonie Brummelkamp, Simon van Velzen and Albertus C. van Raalte, along with their congregations. Ultimately all these seceding ministers were prosecuted, leading them to look towards emigration as possible relief from persecution.

1836   March. First Synodal Meeting, in Amsterdam, of church founded by the seceding ministers; the congregation called itself the Christian Reformed Church.
July 3. Meetings and services of Christian Reformed Church forbidden by proclamation of King William I. The formation of congregations was permitted only if these congregations recognized all the rights of the established Reformed Church. Theoretically a congregation could then be formed by stating its membership and purposes in a petition to the provincial governor, who could approve it and pass it on. In practice, however, such petitions never got past the lowest of local authorities.

1846   April. Van Raalte and Brummelkamp form the Society of Christians for Dutch Immigration to the United States of North America, in Arnhem. There were to be two committees, one in America and one in Holland, which would keep each other informed of their actions. Membership would be open to men 20 or over regardless of their financial standing. The society was to be financed by private gifts; its land would be purchased collectively and all voting members were expected to work on the society's land two days a year for the benefit of the colony. Emigration of the poor would be paid by money raised from private gifts. In May several families were to be sent to investigate land in America. As it turned out, many of the society's rules were not suitable for life in the colony, and were never applied.

Spring. Dominee (Minister) Hendrik P. Scholte finally decided that emigration was spiritually, not just materially necessary, and was therefore not against the will of God.

July. Van Raalte and Brummelkamp published their first pamphlet advocating immigration to America: Immigration, or why we encourage immigration to North America, and not to Java. Included was a discussion of America's more favorable climate, and the fact that Dutch farmers were already acquainted with the kind of crops that could be raised there. Ultimately reprinted three times, the pamphlet contained letters from successful Dutch immigrants in America as well as a discussion of the material difficulties of living in Holland and an appeal for help to Christians living in America.

November. Formation in America of "Netherlands Society for the Protection of Immigrants from Holland", a group of established Americans hoping to protect naive immigrants from unscrupulous persons. The group was largely ineffective, due to the dispersed ports of entry used by the immigrants.

Christmas. Scholte formed the Christian Association for Emigration to North America in Utrecht, whose membership was restricted to non-Catholics of good character. The association's board was to arrange all transportation and negotiate all real estate transactions. 900 people joined.

Almost all the Dutch immigrants between 1845 and 1853 were Seceders. All official attempts to supress the Christian Reformed Church had ended by 1846; it was entirely the example of the ministers and their congregations that started the flow of Seceders to the United States. Ultimately, either as members of an emigration society of independently, more than half of all the Seceders of 1834 left Holland for America.

3.   The Michigan Settlement.   Founding by Van Raalte and Early History.

1846   November 17. The "Southerner" arrives in New York with Van Raalte and 100 members of his Christian Society for Immigration. Rev. Thomas De Witt, of the Reformed Collegiate Church in New York, welcomed them, and on November 18 they sailed up to Albany, where they were received by Rev. Isaac Wyckoff, who had long been active helping Dutch settlers on their way west, and who had read Van Raalte's pamphlets.

1847   January 1. Van Raalte selected the site of his future settlement of Holland in the Black River Country of Fillmore Township, Michigan, near Black Lake, on the site of the Old Wing Mission to the Indians. Michigan had attracted the attention of Hollanders before; Hope and Company, an Amsterdam banking firm, had loaned $1,200,000 to the State of Michigan in 1837 for the building of railroads and canals. Van Raalte picked the Black Lake because of its potential railroad connections, its nearness to the Great Lakes, and the contemporary belief that forest lands were more suitable for farming than prairies.

February 9. Arrival of the first settlers at the site of the Old Wing Mission. The first months were spent in hunger.

March 16. The township of Holland was organized by an act of the Michigan State Legislature.

June. Immigrants from Graafschap ("County") of Bentheim in Hanover, Germany, founded the town of Graafschap southwest of Holland in Laketown and Fillmore townships, Allegan County, Michigan. Bentheim, although technically in Germany, was a region in which the Netherlands dialect and customs prevailed, and in which Calvinism was the dominant religion. Like the Seceders of the Netherlands, these protestants advocated a stricter obedience to Reformed teaching than was approved of by the Hanoverian authorities; Van Raalte himself had once addressed them in Germany.

450 Seceders from the province of Zeeland, in the Netherlands founded the township of Zeeland, northeast of Holland, Michigan. Dominee Cornelius van der Meulen, the leader of the Secession in the province of Zeeland, led the group, which was largely financed by the wealthy Zeeland farmer Jannes van de Luyster, who also subsidized the development of the town after its founding.

Group from the province of Drenthe and from Staphorst in province of Overjjsel settle the community of Drenthe in Zeeland township, southeast of Zeeland. (Drenthe, a purely agricultural area, sent proportionately more settlers to the colony than any other province). The community flourished, and by 1897 was yielding 20,000 lbs. of milk per day.

July. Founding of the community of Vriesland, Michigan, southeast of Zeeland, by a group of Seceders from the province of Friesland, led by Dominee Maarten Anne Ypma.

Entire Holland township was swept by malaria and other diseases for which the Dutch doctor knew no remedy. The illnesses returned the following summer, leaving many dead.

1848   Seceders from province of Drenthe, Overjjsel, Friesland and Groningen found the short-lived village of Groningen, northeast of Holland. The community enjoyed wealth as a lumber and milling center until the forests were depleted of timber around 1895, after which the population declined rapidly.

June. A Group of Seceders led by Dominee Seine Bolks from Hellendoorn in the province of Overijsel founded the community of Hellendoorn, Michigan (later known as Over-ijsel, Mich.), southeast of Holland.

Fall. Jan van Tongeren founded the village of North Holland 5 miles northeast of Holland.

Village of Noordeloos, 1 or 2 miles northeast of North Holland was founded. Named several years later after Noordeloos in the province of South Holland, the home of Dominee Koene van den Bosch, who settled in Michigan in 1856.

1850   Michigan State Constitution gave the franchise to all newcomers who stated their intention to become naturalized and had lived 2 1/2 years in the State. As was to be the case throughout the history of nineteenth and twentieth century Dutch immigration to America, virtually all the settlers wished to become American citizens.

4. The Iowa Settlement. Founding by Scholte and Early History.

1847   May. Scholte arrived in Boston on board the "Sarah Sands". Because he believed his followers, who were used to working in open fields, would more easily adapt to prairie lands, he chose not to join Van Raalte in the forests of Michigan.

July 29. Scholte chose the site for his settlement of Pella in Marion County, Iowa, where he bought about 18,000 acres, many parcels of which possessed houses and barns. The nearest large town was Keokuk, 125 miles away.

August. Founding of Pella, Iowa, so named by Scholte after the city mentioned in Eusebius' Ecclesiastical History as the place of refuge to which the Christians fled after the destruction of Jerusalem because of the wickedness of the Jews. He had chosen for the site the most fertile soil of the Iowa prairie, located on the divide between the Skunk and Des Moines Rivers. The river banks, moreover, were covered with valuable timber, precious on the prairie. Scholte settled the members of his Christian Association for Emigration on the farms and in the dwellings. For those without houses, sod huts were dug in the ground and roofed with grass, a type of dwelling found in the poorer rural regions of the eastern Netherlands. These huts earned the name Straw Town for the Community among the Americans. Unlike the Michigan settlement, Pella

enjoyed prosperity virtually overnight as a cattle an
dairy center, sending to market by the summer of 184
25,000 lbs. of ham and bacon and 5,000 lbs. of lard

1848   January. Lake Praire Township, in which Pella was lo
                cated, absorbed Jefferson township. New arrivals wh
                had declared their intention to become American citizen
                were permitted by a special act of the Iowa State Legisla
                ture to vote for township offices and to run for electio
                to such offices.

                April 21. First township elections in which Lake Prairi
                Township citizens could vote.

1849   June 14. The ship "Franziska" arrived in New Yor
                bringing second large group of immigrants bound for Pella

                Fall. Gold Rush to California brought hundreds throug
                Pella. Dutch settlers made fortunes overnight sellin
                provisions to prospectors.

1850-   600 more immigrants arrive in Pella.
1854

1855   February 1. First issue of Pella Gazette published b
                Scholte, who was as well notary public, attorney, lan
                agent and banker to the community.

1856   Actively encouraged by Scholte, Baptists of Iowa establis
                their Central University in Pella.

        5.   Other Early Settlements in East and Midwest.

           a.   Wisconsin

1834   Father Theodorus van den Broek (born in Amsterdam i
                1783) went to the Fox River region of the Michigan Terri
                tory (an area now located in Wisconsin) to work amon
                the Indians. After he had arrived in America in 1830, Va
                den Broek had studied at the Dominican St. Rose's conven
                in Springfield, Kentucky, and was then sent to St. Joseph'
                convent at Somerset, Ohio to minister to scattered Germa
                Catholics.

1844   First wave of Dutch arrived in Wisconsin, settling mainl
                on the northeast outskirts of Milwaukee (on "Dutch Hill")
                By 1851 the area had around 800 Dutch, and by 1857 th
                entire sixth ward of the city was totally Dutch.

1845   Immigrants from the province of Zeeland under the leadership of Dominie Pieter Zonne settle at Cedar Grove and Oostburg (named for a town in Zeeland Flanders) in Sheboygan County, Wisconsin.

1846   Alto, Wisconsin, founded by Dutch immigrants in Fond du Lac County. By 1859 the grain-raising community had 800 people.

1847   Father Theodorus van den Broek conceived a plan for Dutch Catholic settlement at Little Chute, on the Fox River in Wisconsin, where previous attempts at dams and canals had failed. In the same year he published his Trip to North America in Holland to promote his project.

1848   The ships "Maria Magdalena", "Libera" and "Amerika" arrived from Holland with 350 Catholic immigrants bound for Wisconsin.

1850   Rev. Gerard J. B. van den Heuvel brought 200 Dutch Catholics from Brabant with him to Fox River region of Wisconsin. Ultimately there were to be about 40,000 Dutch Catholic immigrants, but the Fox River region (Green Bay, De Pere, Wrightstown, Kimberly, Combined Locks, Kaukauna, Little Chute and Freedom) was the only really large Catholic colony.

     June. Founding of Hollandtown, Wisconsin, the only entirely Dutch village in the Fox River region, where the Catholics, unlike the Seceders, who remained isolated in communities, mixed easily with their co-religionists, the French Canadians, Germans and Irish.

1853   Oepke Bonnema, a wealthy Dutch grain dealer, founded with his followers the settlement of New Amsterdam, Wisconsin. Not Seceders, but rather members of the established Reformed Church in the Netherlands, these settlers immigrated chiefly for economic reasons. The Community declined after 1880.

1861   A dozen Frisian families founded the town of Friesland, in Columbia County, Wisconsin, 18 miles southwest of Alto. Prosperity came to the community in the 1880's as a result of the building of the tracks of the Northwestern Railroad through that section of Wisconsin. Frisian was still spoken well into the 1930's.

b. Illinois

1847   Founding of Lage Praire, 20 miles south of Chicago, by conservative Reformed immigrants from the province of South Holland (the town was renamed South Holland in 1869), who built up a prosperous farm and dairy center. Further wealth came later in the century, as the community lay on the route of the railroads from Chicago to the south and east.

1848   Many Dutch (not Seceders) settled in southern Chicago, along what is now Roosevelt Road. Because the immigrants were chiefly from the province of Groningen, the area became known as the "Groningen Quarter" (it included the neighborhood of Harrison and May Streets and Halsted Avenue). There was a Reformed Church as early as 1852, but religion in the Quarter did not flourish until the arrival in 1867 of Dominie Bernardus De Bey, who also aided the neighborhood financially. The men of the Quarter were generally employed as teamsters and garbage collectors, some growing rich in these occupations.

1849   Immigrants from the province of North Holland founded Hooge Prairie (later called Roseland), Illinois, six miles north of South Holland. Roseland became famous for its fancy vegetables.

c. Along the Immigrant Trail

1820-   Large group of grain farmers from the province of Zee-
1840   land settled in East Williamson and Pultneyville, N. Y. (vicinity of Rochester). Although not Seceders, these earlier immigrants gave much aid to the later settlers on the way west to the Seceders' colonies in the west.

1835   Klaas Janszoon Beukma of the province of Groningen starts his prosperous farming enterprise near Lafayette, Indiana. Beukma's detailed letters home to Groningen describing his life and growing wealth were widely circulated and attracted a group of Frisians to Indiana in 1847. They give us, moreover, our first picture of life among Groningen immigrants.

1844-   Holland Land Company (see above) brought a group of
1845   Dutch immigrants to settle at its community at Clymer, in Chautauqua County, N. Y.

1846   Wealthy Catholics of the province of Gelderland organized
               a committee for the foundation of a Dutch Catholic colony
               on the Missouri River.

1847   February. 120 Catholics from the province of Gelderland
               sailed to New Orleans with the purpose of founding a Cath-
               olic colony in America, but the group dissolved and scat-
               tered and no trace remains of their activities.

1849   Sayville, 50 miles east of New York City on Long Island,
               attracted a number of Zeelanders acquainted with oyster
               culture. Not Seceders, but Reformed, the immigrants
               were numerous enough to form a congregation by 1866; by
               the 1890's they virtually controlled the oyster business in
               Sayville, several owning entire fishing fleets.

               Worp van Peyma, a wealthy farmer from the province of
               Friesland, founded a small but highly successful dairy
               community at Lancaster, N. Y., which died out only because
               the second generation was lured away to nearby Buffalo.

1853   Seventeen Mennonites from the province of Friesland
               immigrated to America to avoid military service in the
               Netherlands. They settled at New Paris, Indiana, where
               they were quickly absorbed by the other Mennonite groups
               in the vicinity.

1850's   Many hundreds of newly-arrived immigrants, attracted by
               the long-established Reformed congregations and by work
               on the New Jersey waterfront and marshes, settled in Pat-
               erson, Lodi, Passaic and Plainfield, N. J.

        6.   Post Civil War Expansion and Development

               While Dutch immigration declined sharply during the Civil
               War years, it rose steadily after the end of the War, peak-
               ing in 1882, when there were 9,517 immigrants. In 1880
               a new era in Dutch immigration began, due to several fac-
               tors: The population of the Netherlands rose from 4 to
               5 million between 1879 and 1895; Dutch grain farmers
               were no longer able to compete with cheap American and
               Argentine grain; the Holland-America line was founded in
               1873 and reduced the price of the Rotterdam-New York
               fare to ten dollars in 1885; finally, the introduction of
               stiff import tariffs on such Dutch exports as diamonds and
               cigars forced many of their Dutch manufacturers to move
               to America. The financial crises of the 1890's in America
               began to check the flow, although the defeat of the Boers

in 1901 brought a number of South African Dutch to the
United States. The introduction of national immigration
quotas in 1924, however, marked the end of unrestricted
immigration from the Netherlands.

a. Michigan

1860's   Great increase in the Dutch populations of Grand Haven,
              Kalamazoo, Grand Rapids and Muskegon. Musekegon
              ultimately became the largest Groningen community in
              the U. S. Grand Rapids had only 2,000 Dutch before the
              Civil War, but by 1890, it had 10,000 (including second
              generation), with six Reformed churches.

1871   October 8,9. Great Fire of the Dutch settlement at Holland,
              Michigan, destroyed virtually all of Holland, miraculously
              sparing Hope College. Graafschap was also hard hit, with
              damage of $100,000.

              In spite of this setback, the Dutch settlement in Michigan
              gradually expanded to include the whole area between Sau-
              gutuck, Grand Rapids and Muskegon. In 1950 the com-
              bined memberships of the Reformed and Christian Reform-
              ed churches in this area was around 120,000. The whole
              Dutch settlement has become famous for its fancy vege-
              tables, and one of the largest branches of the H. J. Heinz
              Company is in Holland, Michigan.

              Since 1900 small Dutch colonies at Portland, Detroit, Ink-
              ster, Battle Creek and Tulay City, Michigan, have sprung
              up outside the settlement. At the present time the Dutch
              constitute the largest single ethnic group in Western Mich-
              igan.

b. Midwest

1851   Small migration begins from the Netherlands to Mormon
              settlements in Utah. Mainly members of the prophetic
              Zwijndrecht Brotherhood, these immigrants were quickly
              absorbed by the Mormons and did not form independent
              communities. In 1861 two Mormon elders of Dutch descent
              went on the first Mormon mission to the Netherlands and
              were moderately successful among the Zwijndrecht Broth-
              erhood. One of these missionaries, Paul Schettler, trans-
              lated the Book of Mormon into Dutch.

1856-   Fillmore County, Minnesota, settled by Dutch from Alto,
1885   Wisconsin, seeking new farm lands. In 1897 the Reformed
              Church there numbered 60 families.

1866   Minnesota Real Estate Company was founded in Amsterdam. Its aim was to assist holders of St. Paul and Pacific Railroad notes (which had been dumped on the European market) to exchange them for land titles and then to develop the land. This enterprise led to some immigration to Minnesota from the province of South Holland.

1868   Pioneers from Sheboygan County, Wisconsin, founded the town of Holland, Nebraska, 20 miles south of Lincoln in Lancaster County. In spite of the prosperity of Holland, Neb., in the 1880's, Dutch were never attracted to Nebraska in large numbers, partly because of the reputation of the state for heat and drought.

1870   Due to the rise in population and decline in available farm land around Pella, Iowa, the mayor, Henry Hospers, organized a committee for the colonization of northwest Iowa. Holland, Iowa, later re-named Orange City, was founded in 1871, and by 1873 had 400 families.

1874   Arrival in Newton and Alexanderwohl, Kansas, of a group of Russian Mennonites who were seeking to escape military service in Russia. They were descendants of Dutch Mennonites who had left the province of Groningen in the 17th century, settling in West Prussia, then Russia. They were attracted to Kansas by a special act of the State Legislature exempting them from the draft.

1882   Dutch pioneers from Orange City, Iowa, settled in Douglas and Charles Mix Counties, South Dakota, and establish hog ranches. By 1885 the counties contained 3,000 Dutch.

1885   Emmons County, North Dakota, and Campbell County, South Dakota, settled by Dutch pioneers from Michigan.

1888   Prinsburg, Minnesota founded and named after Martin Prins of the province of Groningen, head of a Chicago real estate firm which encouraged Dutch settlements along the route of the Chicago, St. Paul and Milwaukee Railroad lines.

1892   Reformed minister Andreas Wormser, a Dutch-born graduate of Hope College, led a group of Dutch immigrants to settle Manhattan, Montana, which had 85 Dutch families by 1911.

        c.   Far West, South and Southwest

1867   Under the encouragement of Van Raalte, who hoped to establish another large Dutch settlement like the one in Michigan somewhere in the South, 80 Michigan Dutch and a large group of Netherlanders settled at Amelia County, Va., 25 miles southwest of Richmond. In 1870 Van Raalte founded the Amelia Institute, modelled after Holland Academy in Michigan. Ultimately three Reformed congregations were formed. Due to the lack of jobs locally and to the crop failure of 170, the community disintegrated and all trace of it was lost after 1876.

1875

John Verboort led six Roman Catholic Dutch families to found the first permanent Dutch community on the West Coast in Oregon. The settlement, called Verboort, was 3 miles northeast of Forest Grove, consisting mainly of Dutch from the Fox River Valley region of Wisconsin.

1870's-
1890's

Myriad attempts by Dutch-American real estate enterprises to establish communities in California, Montana, Oregon and Utah. Generally the Dutch settlers were sadly disappointed by the difference between the conditions they found and the conditions they had been promised, and the communities usually disintegrated in disillusionment.

1880's-
1890's

Construction of Kansas City Southern Railroad (from Kansas City to Port Arthur, Texas), in which Dutch capital played an essential role. Dutch names were given to stations along this route, including Amsterdam, Mo., Vandervoort, Ark., and Nederland, Tex. In general, Dutch financial interests had no connection with Dutch immigration, and there is no reason to believe that Dutch workmen were employed in the building of the Kansas City Southern.

1890's

A succession of crop failures in the Dakotas and in Montana began a large scale Dutch immigration to Washington State, which was encouraged by the Northern Pacific Railroad.

1896

Largest Dutch settlement in Washington State established at Lynden in the Nooksack Valley.

1925

A. M. Welling organized settlement of a large number of mainly second generation Dutch at Terra Ceia on Pamlico Sound, North Carolina. By 1943 the Christian Reformed congregation there numbered 70 people, making Terra Ceia one of the only permanent Dutch colonies in the South, which, initially because of the slavery issue but ultimately because of the climate, has remained unattractive to Dutch settlement.

III.   The Dutch Immigrants' Cultural Experience and Contribution

    A.   Religion

        1.   Protestants

1850

June 5. The General Synod of the Reformed Church in America voted to accept as member churches the Seceders' congregations in Wisconsin and in Van Raalte and Scholte's settlements. This merger meant that the immigrants' churches would now receive financial help from the rich eastern churches and could train their ministers at the New Brunswick Theological Seminary; it means additionally that the process of Americanization was greatly accelerated among members of these churches; by the end of the 1850's English had gained a foothold in their services.

1857

Dominie Koene van den Bosch of Noordeloos, Michigan, withdraws his congregation from the Reformed Church in America in protest against the laxity in its practices, thus beginning the Secession in America. The Seceders of 1857 objected among other things to the Reformed Church's tendency to ignore the doctrine of predestination, its failure to insist on weekly readings from the Heidelberg Catechism, and, above all, to its tolerance of membership in Masonic lodges.

1864

American Seceders adopt the name True Dutch Reformed Church, after some congregations that seceded from the American church in 1822, but in 1890 they changed their name again to Christian Reformed Church. Cut off from the rich congregations in the east, the Christian Reformed Church had great financial difficulties and in 1879 had only 17 ministers.

1882

The Christian Reformed Church in the Netherlands (those Seceders of 1834 who had not immigrated) had been initially critical of the True Dutch Reformed Church and remained loyal to Van Raalte's merger with the Reformed Church in America. In 1882, however, the question of Freemasonry arose and the Reformed Church defended its liberal attitude towards membership; the Christian Reformed Church in the Netherlands consequently broke with the Reformed church in America and went over to the True Dutch Reformed church. From then on most Dutch immigrants, who were mainly Christian Reformed in the Netherlands, joined the True Dutch (later Christian Reformed) Church in America, meaning that the use of Dutch persisted much longer in services than it did in the Reformed Church. By 1950,

however, only a few Christian Reformed congregations still
used Dutch, and then only in special services conducted for
the elderly.

1890   The original True Dutch Reformed Church, of Hackensack,
N. J., which had seceded from the Reformed Church in
America in 1822, merged with the Christian Reformed
Church. The totally Americanized New Jersey congregations, descended from 17th century Dutch immigrants,
were an important factor in the growth of the use of English in Christian Reformed services.

2. Roman Catholic

1851   Fathers van den Broek and van den Heuvel founded the first
house of the Crusade Fathers (Cruciferi) in Little Chute,
Wisconsin, with assistance from the Canons Regular of the
Order of the Holy Cross, whose mother house was in Cuyck,
in the province of North Brabant in the Netherlands. The
Crusade Fathers founded the Crosier Seminary in Onamia,
Minnesota, and were active in the Catholic Colonization So-
ciety of the United States of America.

1907   Many of the Dutch Catholics who immigrated to America
settled on farms far from established Catholic Churches;
some of these invariably drifted from the faith. In order to
stop this tendency towards dispersal, the Association of
Belgian and Dutch Priests was set up in Chicago in 1907.
In 1911 it was absorbed by the Catholic Colonization Society
of the United States of America which had a Dutch and
Flemish branch sponsored by the archbishop of St. Louis
and the bishop of Milwaukee. The purpose of the Society
was to provide land companies with suitable immigrant settlers in return for the land company's promise to support a
priest to serve the new communities. Settlements, mainly
consisting of Brabanters and Limburgers, were organized
at Butler, Minn., and in Dunklin County, Mo.

B. The Dutch-American Press

1849   October 16. Jacob Quintus, of the province of Zeeland, began publishing De Sheboygan Nieuwsbode, the first successful Dutch language weekly newspaper. Quintus chose
Sheboygan because its location facilitated distribution to
the Michigan, Wisconsin and Iowa settlements. The
Nieuwsbode's politics vaccillated between the Republican
and Democratic parties until it merged with the Sheboygan
Zeitung in 1860.

1850   Fall. Van Raalte began publication of De Hollander (half in Dutch, half in English) for the Michigan Settlement. By 1856 the paper was completely in Dutch; until it ceased publication in 1894 De Hollander was always a Democratic paper.

1852   May. First issue of Giles van der Wall's De Nederlander in Kalamazoo, a Whig newspaper which ceased publication after the November elections.

1855   February 1. Scholte started publication of the English language Pella Gazette, which was forced to suspend publication in 1860 due to lack of money.

1859   The Dutch language Democratic newspaper De Amerikansche Stoompost brought out by Quintus in Grand Rapids, Michigan, and continued publication until 1866.

1859   Spring. C. G. van Altena and S. H. Salverda began publication of their pro-Republican De Ware Burger, which contained one column of news in English. It ceased publication in October, 1859.

1860   April 30. First issue of De Grondwet, published by Jan Roost, originally of Harderwijk in the Netherlands. Because the only Dutch newspaper to survive until 1860 (De Hollander) was Democratic, Roost started his Grondwet to fill the need for a conservative Republican Dutch newspaper. It ultimately became the most influential Dutch publication in America.

1862   The first issue of the Republican weekly De Hope, originally published by Jan Binnekant as De Verzamelaar; it became De Hope in 1865. Its policies were directed by the faculty of Hope College, and it survived until the late 1920's as the official voice of the Reformed Church in the midwest.

1868   November. Publication began in Grand Rapids of Vrijheids Banier, which survived until 1900.

            C. Vorst and Dominie Douwe van der Werp started the weekly publication of De Wachter to spread the Christian Reformed movement. It has remained the official organ of the Church.

1874   Henry Hospers began publication of the Republican, orthodox Christian De Volksvriend in Orange City, Iowa. In 1909 it had a subscription list of 4,000.

1875	De Standaard-Bulletin, a very successful Christian Reformed, Republican news weekly, began publication in Grand Rapids, Michigan. It survived until the 1930's.
1878	Roman Catholic-oriented De Pere (Wisc.) Standaard begins publication.
1882	In Paterson, N. J., De Telegraaf began publication and survived well into the 20th century.
1888	The ultra-orthodox Christian, conservative Republican weekly De Hollandsche Amerikaan began appearing in Kalamazoo, Michigan.
1880's	In the Dakotas, De Nederlandsche Dakotiaan and De Harrison Bode were published briefly but enjoyed little success.
	In Chicago the Republican weekly De Nederlander was published by J. Esnorff until 1893, when it was bought out by De Grondwet, which suspended the publication of De Nederlander and brought out instead a special edition of De Grondwet for Chicago.
1892	Appearance of the Republican newsweekly De Sioux Center Nieuwsblad.
1896	Eduard van der Casteele brought out the first issues of the Catholic Onze Standaard.
	Bilingual monthly De Heidenwereld (The Pagan World) begun in Orange City, Iowa, by Reformed and Christian Reformed Churches working together.
1897	The beginning of the publication in Chicago of Onze Toekomst, a small Republican, Christian Reformed weekly whose political views were strictly tied to orthodox teaching.
1890's	Brief appearance in the Dakotas of De Springfield Bode.
1904	First issues in Paterson, N. J., of Het Oosten (The East), which continued for several decades as an ultra-orthodox Christian publication.
1908	De Gazette van Moline (Ill.) began publication as an independent Flemish Catholic new weekly.

1909   De Volksvriend of Muskegon, Mich., began appearing, and at its height had 400 subscribers.

1914   The first issues of weekly De Utah Nederlander appear as the Republican, Dutch-language organ of the Mormon Church.

1917   Jan van Boven published De Tekenen der Tijden (Signs of the Times), a Republican Christian news weekly, in Kalamazoo, Michigan.

1919   Merger of John B. Heyrman's Catholic De Volkstem (De Pere, Wisc.) with De Gazette van Moline, which then merged with De Gazette van Detroit. The Gazettes were geared almost entirely to a Flemish Catholic audience. The Gazette van Detroit is still being published.

C.   Political Activity

1852   First national elections in which the immigrants of 1846 were able to vote, due to the liberal state laws extending the franchise to new arrivals who declared their intention to become naturalized. The immigrants voted overwhelmingly Democratic, understandably enough, as the Democratic Party of the time was still that of Jackson's populist sympathies; it supported, moreover, liberal immigration laws and the early extention of the franchise to immigrants. Later in the decade, however, many Dutch split with the Democrats over the issue of slavery and joined the Republicans, who were abolitionists. The effect of the Civil War was to make most Dutch Republicans, which they remained for some years thereafter.

1884   Arrival in the U. S. of Daniel De Leon (1852-1914), A Dutch subject born in Curacao and educated in Amsterdam, De Leon joined the Knights of Labor in 1888. He was a leading force in the Socialist Labor Party in the 1890's and in 1905 helped found the Industrial Workers of the World. De Leon's activities were not known to the mass of Dutch immigrants, who had been taught by their orthodox religious leaders to abhore socialism as unchristian. Their refusal to strike for decent wages and their general passivity in the face of economic exploitation led to great resentment of the Dutch by other industrial workers (especially in Grand Rapids), who regarded the Dutch as scabs and strikebreakers.

1898

Chicagoan J. Hoddenbach van Scheltema, originally of Arnhem, founded the General Dutch League (Algemeen Nederlandsch Verbond) to stimulate Dutch patriotism among immigrants. By collecting signatures at the Chicago World's Fair of 1893 he managed to secure enough support to begin publication of the League's Neerlandia, a magazine dedicated to the propagation (and glorification) of Dutch culture. The first issue (July 11, 1896) appeared on the anniversary of the Battle of the Golden Spurs at Courtrai, when the flower of the French nobility was defeated by an alliance of Flemish artisans. The League ultimately had active branches in New York, Roseland and Chicago, Ill., Grand Rapids, Muskegon and Zeeland, Mich., and Fulton and Pella, Iowa.

Coronation of Wilhelmina, at 18 the first Queen of the Netherlands and the Indies, additionally stimulated a sense of nationalism among the Dutch immigrants.

1899-
1902

The Boer War in South Africa. The American Dutch enthusiastically supported the Boers, with whom they identified not only because of their common national origins but because of their common orthodox Calvinism. Demonstrations were held, at which money for the Boers was raised, and a petition was presented to President McKinley asking him to negotiate with the warring parties. Cables were sent to London denouncing the British for alleged atrocities in South Africa, and children wore "Oom Paul" buttons in honor of President Kruger of the Transvaal Republic. After their defeat by the British a number of Boers came to America, where they generally became members of the Christian Reformed Church.

1914
1918

During the first World War the Netherlands remained neutral, which was widely (and falsely) taken by rabid American patriots to mean that it sympathized with Germany. There was also a great deal of genuine confusion of the two national groups by many Americans, who used the terms "Dutch" and "German" interchangeably (the Pennsylvania Dutch, for example, were Germans, i. e. "deutsche"). A Dutch school in Iowa was set afire and a few Dutch street names were changed. A large number of Dutch immigrants who wanted there to be no question about their Americanism began consciously to abandon those aspects of their life style which were most obviously foreign; Dutch was spoken less frequently in the home, church services went over to English, people Americanized their family names and gave their children common English first names.

1938

The Christian Labor Association was founded in Grand Rapids, Mich., by members of the Christian Reformed Church who felt that the conflicts between capital and labor could be resolved by the judicious application of Christian principles. Opposed to strikes or disorder of any kind, the Labor Association states in its constitution that "injustices in the social and economic system are due to the disregard of divinely instituted laws". In 1947, when the Association counted several thousand members, it began publishing the Christian Labor Herald to advocate a labor program based on the principles of social justice found in the Bible.

D. Education

1770

Establishment of Queens College (later Rutgers College) at New Brunswick, New Jersey, by Reformed Church. Rather than send their aspiring ministers to Presbyterian Princeton College, the Reformed Church fathers founded their own institution, to which they added a theological seminary in 1810.

1795

Founding of Union College in Schenectady, N. Y. by the Reformed Church to prepare its aspiring ministers for further work at New Brunswick.

1851

Hope Academy in Holland, Mich., began instruction, funded by monies sent by the Reformed Churches in the east for the purpose of preparing the sons of the Dutch colonists to enter Rutgers College. The Academy's first building was completed in 1856.

1857

The Reformed Classis of Holland, Mich., founded the first "Christian School" to teach children elementary subjects according to the principles of Reformed doctrine. These schools spread throughout the Dutch settlements, greatly encouraged by Dr. Abraham Kuyper, the leader of orthodox Reformed teaching in the Netherlands. Supported financially by private gifts, the Christian Schools were attached to specific church congregations, similar to Catholic parochial schools. Now they are mainly elementary institutions of the Christian Reformed Church. In 1921 the schools began publishing the magazine Christian Home and School, which discussed pedagogy in the Christian Schools.

1866

Founding of Hope College with the aid of $40,000 sent from the Reformed Churches in the east. The Rev. Philip Phelps was its first president. In 1867 a theology professorship was established, with a theology department under the council of Hope College, although in 1877 instruction in that department was suspended because of lack of funds. In 1884 the theology division was re-established as the separate Western Theological Seminary of the Reformed Church.

1876   Calvin Theological Seminary of the Christian Reformed Church was founded. The immigration of the 1880's swelled the ranks of the Christian Reformed Church, and it was hoped that the new school would develop along the pattern of the Free University of Amsterdam, which was founded in 1880 by the Christian Reformed Church in the Netherlands. A great expansion of the curriculum took place around World War I, and in 1920 the institution was accredited to bestow the Bachelor of Arts degree as Calvin College.

1912   Establishment of a chair in Dutch History, Literature and Art at the University of Chicago. Dutch funds were used to found the chair, on the understanding that the cost of the Lectureship would eventually be assumed by the university. The first and only incumbent was Temen De Vries, a graduate of the Free University of Amsterdam who had been active in Christian Reformed politics in the Netherlands. The chair was discontinued in 1914.

1913   Establishment of the Queen Wilhelmina Lectureship at Columbia University, funded by 35,000 guilders given by Netherlanders associated with the General Dutch League. This contribution was matched by the university. More recently the Dutch Government has taken on half the financial obligations of the chair. The Lecturers are nominated by the Dutch Ministry of Education and appointed by the university. The first Lecturer was Leonard Charles van Noppen, who had immigrated to North Carolina from the Netherlands as a boy, and who was known for his translation of Vondel's Lucifer. Since the Queen Wilhelmina Lecturers have been Adriaan Barnouw, a philologist, Benjamin Hunningher, a theater historian, and the present incumbent, J. W. Smit, an historian of the European Reformation.

1916   Central College in Pella, Iowa, was taken over by the Reformed Church in America. Originally founded in 1856 by the Baptists with the encouragement of Scholte, Central University, as it was then known, failed to flourish. After the Reformed take-over, however, it rapidly expanded, providing an alternative to Hope College in the midwest.

1953   Establishment of the Queen Juliana Chair of Dutch Lan-
            guage and Culture at Calvin College upon the occasion of
            the Queen's visit to the College in that year.

1967   The Erasmus Lectureship was founded at Harvard Uni-
            versity, to bring Dutch scholars to teach in American on
            an annual basis.

1971   The foundation of the Princess Beatrix Lectureship for
            the teaching of Dutch language and literature at the Uni-
            versity of California at Berkeley. In recent years, Dutch
            lectureships have also been established at the University
            of Michigan at Ann Arbor, and the University of Texas.

        E. Literature

1652   Jacob Steendam (1616-1672) arrived in New Amsterdam,
            where he was active as a poet until his departure for Java
            in 1660. His poems, some of which were written to en-
            courage Dutch immigration to New Netherland (he wrote,
            for example, for Plockhoy's pamphlets), include "The
            Complaint of New Amsterdam in New Netherland to her
            Mother" (1659), and "In Praise of New Netherland" (1661).

1870   Edward Bok immigrated at the age of 6 from Den Helder.
            Editor of The Ladies Home Journal in the first decades of
            this century, and friend of Theodore Roosevelt, Bok wrote
            The Americanization of Edward Bok, and The Autobio-
            graphy of a Dutch Boy Fifty Years After, which appeared
            in 1920, was in 1923 one of the four most read works of
            non-fiction and which was in its 37th printing by 1926.

1913   Arnold Mulder's first novel, Dominie of Harlem (Chicago,
            1913) appeared, attacking the religious orthodoxy of the
            early Dutch settlers. His subsequent novels, Bram of the
            Five Corners (Chicago, 1915) and The Outbound Road (Bos-
            ton, 1919) the Dutch-American communities.

1919   Appearance of D. Nieland's Yankee Dutch: Humoristische
            Schetsen uit het Hollandsch-Amerikaansche Volksleven
            (Grand Rapids, 1919). Nieland's humorous tales demon-
            strate the utter degeneration of the Dutch language in the
            midwest. His 'n Fonnie Bisnis (Grand Rapids 1947) is
            in the same genre.

1930   H. K. Pasma, a Frisian who immigrated as a boy with his
            parents to Wilhelmina, Maryland, published his reminis-
            cences, Close-Hauled (New York, 1930).

1936　　　　　John van Lieuwen published his first volume of Dutch dialect humor, Troebel en Fon, followed in 1947 by Swet en Tears. The poems in these volumes are written in prairie Dutch, hardly recognizable to the native Netherlander.

1943　　　　　David C. De Jong published his Belly Fulla Straw (New York, 1943), an account of his family's experiences as Frisian immigrants, followed by his own autobiography, With a Dutch Accent (New York, 1944).

1945　　　　　Publication of Sara Gosselink's Roofs Over Strawtown (Grand Rapids, 1945), an historical account of the early days of Pella, Iowa.

1946　　　　　Appearance of J. Keuning's The Man in Bearskin (Grand Rapids, 1946), a fictional account of the original Van Raalte group and the early years of the Michigan settlement.

1951　　　　　Appearance of Jan de Hertog's play "The Fourposter", which was subsequently made into a movie of the same title and formed the basis for the hit Broadway musical "I Do! I Do!. De Hertog, who was born in Haarlem, province of North Holland, on April 22, 1914, is the most successful Dutch-American writer to date. His many works include the novel The Spiral Road, which appeared in 1957 and was made into a movie starring Rock Hudson.

1968　　　　　Appearance of John Updike's best-selling novel, Couples. The hero of Couples, like Updike, comes of rigidly religious Dutch immigrant stock, and his background in the Dutch colony forms an important aspect of this novel. Updike himself was born in 1932 and is the author also of Rabbit Run (1960) and The Centaur (1963).

DOCUMENTS

GRANT OF EXCLUSIVE TRADE TO NEW NETHERLAND.
From the Minute on a half sheet of paper, in the Royal Archieves in the Hague; File, Loopende.

The States General of the United Netherlands to all to whom these presents shall come, Greeting. Whereas Gerrit Jacobz Witssen, antient Burgomaster of the City Amsterdam, Jonas Witssen, Simon Morrissen, owners of the Ship named the Little Fox whereof Jan de With has been Skipper; Hans Hongers, Paulus Pelgrom, Lanbrecht van Tweenhuyzen, owners of the two ships named the Tiger and the Fortune, whereof Aedriaen Block and Henrick Corstiaenssen were Skippers; Arnolt van Lybergen, Wessel Schenck, Hans Claessen and Berent Sweertssen, owners of the Ship named the Nightingale, whereof Thys Volckertssen was Skipper, Merchants of the aforesaid City Amstelredam, and Pieter Clementssen Brouwer, Jan Clementssen Kies, and Cornelis Volckertssen, Merchants of the City of Hoorn, owners of the Ship named the Fortuyn, whereof Cornelis Jacobssen May was Skipper, all now associated in one company, have respectfully represented to us, that they, the petitioners, after great expenses and damages by loss of ships and other dangers, had, during the present year, discovered and found with the above named five ships, certain New Lands situate in America, between New France and Virginia, the Sea coasts whereof lie between forty and forty five degrees of Latitude, and now called New Netherland: And whereas We did, in the month of March last, for the promotion and increase of Commerce, cause to be published a certain General Consent and Charter setting forth, that whosoever should thereafter discover new havens, lands, places or passages, might frequent, or cause to be frequented, for four voyages, such newly discovered and found places, passages, havens, or lands, to the exclusion of all others from visiting or frequenting the same from the United Netherlands, until the said first discoverers and finders shall, themselves, have completed the said four Voyages, or caused the same to be done within the time prescribed for that purpose, under the penalties expressed in the said Octroy &c. they request that we would accord to them due Act of the aforesaid Octroy in the usual form:

Which being considered, We, therefore, in Our Assembly having the pertinent Report of the Petitioners, relative to the discoveries and finding of the said new Countries between the above named limits and degrees, and also of their adventures, have consented and granted, and by these presents do consent and grant, to the said Petitioners now united into one Company, that they shall be privileged exclusively to frequent or cause to be visited, the above newly discovered lands, situate in America between New France and Virginia, whereof the Sea coasts lie between the fortieth and forty fifth degrees of Latitude, now named New Netherland, as can be seen by a Figurative Map hereunto annexed, and that for four Voyages within the term of three Years, commencing the first of January, Sixteen hundred and fifteen next ensuing, or sooner, without it being permitted to any other person from the United Netherlands, to sail to, navigate or frequent the said newly discovered lands, havens or places, either directly or indirectly, within

37

the said three Years, on pain of Confiscation of the vessel and Cargo wherewith infraction hereof shall be attempted, and a fine of Fifty thousand Netherland Ducats for the benefit of said discoverers or finders; provided, nevertheless, that by these presents We do not intend to prejudice or diminish any of our former grants or Charters; And it is also Our intention, that if any disputes or differences arise from these Our Concessions, they shall be decided by Ourselves.

We therefore expressly command all Governors, Justices, Officers, Magistrates and inhabitants of the aforesaid United Countries, that they allow the said Company peaceably and quietly to enjoy the whole benefit of this Our grant and consent, ceasing all contradictions and obstacles to the contrary. For such we have found to appertain to the public service. Given under Our Seal, paraph and signature of our Secretary at the Hague the xi[th] of October 1614.

DOCUMENTS RELATING TO THE DUTCH IN AMERICA

Mr. Peter Schagen to the States General; the Island of Manhattans purchased

High and Mighty Lords:

Yesterday, arrived here the Ship the Arms of Amsterdam, which sailed from New Netherland, out of the River Mauritius, on the 23rd September. They report that our people are in good heart and live in peace there; the Women also have borne some children there. They have purchased the Island Manhattes from the Indians for the value of 60 guilders; 'tis 11,000 morgens in size. They had all their grain sowed by the middle of May, and reaped by the middle of August. They send thence samples of summer grain; such as wheat, rye, barley, oats, buckwheat, canary seed, beans and flax.

The cargo of the aforesaid ship is:---7246 Beaver skins.
                           178 1/2 Otter skins.
                           675 Otter skins.
                           48 Minck skins.
                           36 Wild cat skins.
                           33 Mincks.
                           34 Rat skins.

Considerable Oak timber and Hickory.
Herewith, High and Mighty Lords, be commended to the mercy of the Almighty.

In Amsterdam, the 5th November, Ad 1626.   Your High Mightinesses'
Received 7th November, 1626.   obedient,
                                         (Signed)   P. Schagen.

The address was as follows:
    High and Mighty Lords,
    My Lords the States General
    at the Hague.

Patent to Kiliaen Van Rensselaer for a Tract of Land on Hudson's River.

Anno 1630, adi 13th of August. We, the Director and Council of New Netherland, residing on the Island Manhatas and in Fort Amsterdam, under the authority of their High Mightinesses the Lords States General of the United Netherlands and the Incorporated West India Company, Chamber at Amsterdam, do hereby acknowledge and declare, that on this day, the date underwritten, before us appeared and presented themselves in their proper persons: Kottomack, Nawanemit Albantzeene, Sagiskwa and Kanaomack, owners and proprietors of their respective parcels of land, extending up the River, South and North, from said Fort unto a little south of Moeneminnes Castle, to the aforesaid proprietors, belonging jointly and in common, and the aforesaid Nawanemit's particular land called Semesseerse, lying on the East Bank opposite Castle Island off unto the above mentioned Fort; Item, from Petanock, the Millstream, away North to Negagonse, in extent about three miles, and declared freely and advisedly for and on account of certain parcels of Cargoes, which they acknowledge to have received in their hands and power before the execution hereof, and, by virtue and bill of sale, to hereby transport, convey and make over to the Mr. Kiliaen van Rensselaer, absent, and for whom We, ex officio and with due stipulation, accept the same; namely: the respective parcels of land hereinbefore specified, with the timber, appendencies and dependencies thereof, together with all the action, right and jurisdiction to them the grantors conjointly or severally belonging, constituting and surrogating the said Mr. Rensselaer in their stead, state and right, real and actual possession thereof, and at the same time giving him full, absolute and irrevocable power authority and special command to hold, in quiet possession, cultivation, occupancy and use, tanquam actor et procurator in rem suam ac propriam, the land aforesaid, acquired by said Mr. Van Rensselaer, or those who may hereafter acquire his interest; also, to dispose of, do with and alienate it, as he or others should or might do with his other and own Lands and domains acquired by good and lawful title, without the grantors therein retaining, reserving or holding any, the smallest part, right, action or authority whether of property, command or jurisdiction, but rather, hereby, desisting, retiring and renouncing therefrom forever, for the behoof aforesaid; further promising this their conveyance and whatever may by virtue thereof be done, not only forever to hold fast and irrevocable, to observe and to fulfill, but also to give security for the surrender of the aforesaid land, obligans et renuncians a bona fide. In testimony is this confirmed by our usual signature, with the ordinary seal thereunto depending. Done at the aforesaid Island Manahatas and Fort Amsterdam, on the day and year aforesaid. Signed, Peter Minuit, Director; Pieter Bylvelt, Jacob Elbertss. Wissinck, Jan Jassen Brouwer, Symon Dirckss. Pos, Reyner Harmensen, Jan Lampe, Sheriff.

There was, besides: This Conveyance written with mine own hand is, in consequence of the Secretary's absence, executed in my presence on the

thirteenth day of August, XVI, and thirty, as above.   Signed, Lenart Cole,
Deputy Secretary.

After collating with the Original, dated, signed and sealed as above,
this Copy is found to agree with it.   Amsterdam, the 5th September, 1672.

In testimony,   (Signed)   Adriaen Lock,
                                          Notaris Publ.
                                          1672.

PROPOSED FREEDOMS AND EXEMPTIONS
FOR NEW NETHERLAND. 1640.

From the Original, in the Royal Archives at the Hague;
File, West Indie.

Freedoms and Exemptions granted and accorded by the Directors
of the General Incorporated West India Company at the Assembly
of the XIX., with the approbation of the High and Mighty Lords
States General of the free United Netherlands, to all Patroons,
Masters, or Private persons who will plant any Colonies or intro-
duce cattle in New Netherland. Exhibited 19th July, 1640.

All good inhabitants of the Netherlands and all others inclined to plant
any Colonies in New Netherland shall be at liberty to send three or four
persons in the Company's ships going thither, to examine the circumstances
there, on condition that they swear to the articles, as well as the officers
and seamen, as far as they relate to them, and pay for board and passage
out and home, to wit, those who eat in the master's cabin, fifteen stivers
per day, and those who go and eat in the orlop, shall have their board and
passage gratis, and in case of an attack, offensive or defensive, they shall
be obliged to lend a hand with the others, on condition of receiving, should
any of the enemy's ships be overcome, their share of the booty pro rata,
each according to his quality, to wit---the Colonists eating out of the Cabin
shall be rated with the seamen, and those eating in the cabin with the Company's servants who board there and have the lowest rate of pay.

In the selection of lands, those who shall have first notified and presented themselves to the Company, whether Patroons or private Colonists,
shall be preferred to others who may follow.

In case any one be deceived in selecting ground, or should the place
by him chosen afterwards not please him, he will, upon previous represent-
ation to the Governor and Council then be at liberty to select another situation.

For Patroons and Feudatories of New Netherland, shall be acknowledged all such as shall ship hence, and plant there a Colonie of fifty souls,
above fifteen years of age, within the space of three years after having made
a declaration and given notice thereof, to some Chamber of the company
here or to the Governor or Council there; namely, one-third part within
the year, and so forth, from year to year, until the number be completed; on
pain of losing, through notorious neglect, the obtained Freedoms and cattle.
But they shall be warned that the Company reserves the Island Manhattes
to itself.

All Patroons and Feudatories shall, on requesting it, be granted Venia
Testandi, or the power to dispose of, or bequeath, his fief by Will.

42

For Masters or Colonists, shall be acknowledged, those who will remove to New Netherland with five souls above fifteen years; to all such,
our Governor there shall grant in property one hundred morgens, Rhineland measure, of land, contiguous one to the other, wherever they please
to select.

And the Patroons, of themselves or by their agents, at the places
where they will plant their Colonies, shall have the privilege to extend the
latter one mile (consisting of, or estimated at, 1600 Rhineland perches)
along the coast, bay, or a navigable river, and two contiguous miles land-
ward in; it being well understood, that no two Patroonships shall be selected on both sides of a river or bay, right opposite to each other; and that
the Company retains to itself the property of the lands lying between the
limits of the Colonies, to dispose thereof hereafter according to its pleasure; and that the Patroons and Colonists shall be obliged to give each other
an outlet and issue, (uytteweghen ende uyttewateren) at the nearest place
and at the smallest expense; and in case of disagreement, it shall be settled in the presence and by the decision of the Governor for the time being.

The Patroons shall forever possess all the lands situate within their
limits, together with the produce, superficies, minerals, rivers and foun-
tains thereof, with high, low and middle jurisdiction, hunting, fishing, fow-
ling and milling, the lands remaining allodial, but the jurisdiction as of a
perpetual hereditary fief, devolvable by death as well to females as to
males, and fealty and homage for which is to be rendered to the Company, on each of such occasions, with a pair of iron gauntlets, redeemable by
twenty guilders within a year and six weeks, at the Assembly of the XIX.,
here, or before the Governor there; with this understanding, that in case
of division of said fief or jurisdiction, be it high, middle or low, the parts
shall be and remain of the same nature as was originally conferred on the
whole, and fealty and homage must be rendered for each part thereof by a
pair of iron gauntlets, redeemable by twenty guilders, as aforesaid.

And should any Patroon, in course of time, happen to prosper in his
Colonie to such a degree as to be able to found one or more towns, he shall
have authority to appoint officers and magistrates there, and make use of
the title of his Colonie, according to the pleasure and the quality of the
persons, all saving the Company's regalia.

And should it happen that the dwelling places of private Colonists
become so numerous as to be accounted towns, villages or cities, the
Company shall give orders respecting the subaltern government, magistrates and ministers of justice, who shall be nominated by the said towns
and villages in a triple number of the best qualified, from which a choice
and selection is to be made by the Governor and Council; and those shall
determine all questions and suits within their district.

The Patroons who will send Colonies thither, shall furnish them with
due instruction agreeably to the mode of government both in police and
justice established, or to be established, by the Assembly of the XIX, which
they shall first exhibit to the Directors of the respective Chambers, and
have approved by the Assembly of the XIX.

The Patroons and Colonists shall have the privilege of sending their people and property there in the Company's ships, on condition of swearing allegiance, and paying to the Company for the conveyance of the people, as in the first article, and for freight of the goods requisite for their bouwery, five per cent on the cost of the goods here, without, however, including herein the cattle, on the freight of which the Company shall be liberal.

But in case it should come to pass that the Company have no ships to dispatch, or that there be no room in the sailing vessels, in such a case the Patroons and Colonists can, upon previously communicating their determination to, and obtaining the consent of the Company in writing, send their own ships thither, provided, in going and returning, they shall not leave the ordinary track laid down, and take a supercargo, whose board shall be at the expense of the Patroons or Colonists, and whose wages shall be paid by the Company; on pain, in case of contravention, of forfeiting their ship and goods to, and for the behalf of, the Company, it remaining optional with the Patroons, during the term of the current grant, and no longer, to convey over their cattle, wares and people in the Company's ships, in their own or in chartered vessels.

And, whereas, it is the Company's intention first to settle the Island of the Manhattes, it shall provisionally be the staple of all produce and wares accruing on the North river and the country thereabout, before they can be sent further, except those which by nature itself are useless there, or cannot be brought there except with great loss to the owners, in which case the latter shall be bound to give timely notice of such inconvenience to the Company here, or to the Governor and Council there, that it be provided for, according as the circumstances shall be found to require.

All Patroons, Colonists and inhabitants there, as well as the stockholders in the Company here, shall be privileged to sail and trade to the entire coast, from Florida to Newfoundland, on the following conditions:

First, that all goods which will be sent hence for sale there, whether freighted by the Company, or by Colonists, or the stockholders themselves, must be brought into the Company's stores for inspection and payment of the proper duties, to wit: ten per cent on the cash cost of the article here, besides convoy-freight and average, an agreement being made for the freights of what may be sent in the Company's ships; and bulk will not be allowed to be broken any where except at the Manhattes, or such place as the Company here may order, so as to be at liberty, after proper inspection of their loading and the entry thereof, to depart to whatever place they think proper.

And on the other wares which will be sent thence hither, shall be paid here, over and above the convoy duty granted by the State to the Company, five per cent, according to the valuation to be made here, on such penalty as aforesaid; but an agreement must be made with the Governor and Council there, for the freight of any of the goods that are being sent from there here, shall be paid to the Governor and Council there, ten per cent, all in kind, and due receipt for the payment thereof, shall be brought along, on pain of confiscation of all the furs which will be found not to have paid anything for the behoof of the Company, and with that to be exempt from further duty.

And in case said private ships, in going or coming, or in ranging along the coast from Florida to Newfoundland, happen to capture any prizes, they shall, in like manner be obliged to bring the same, or to cause the same to be brought, to the Governor and Council in New Netherland, or to the Chamber whence they respectively sailed, to be rewarded by them, and the third part thereof shall be retained for the Company, before deducting his Highness' and the State's portion, the two other third parts for themselves, in return for their incurred expenses and risk, all in pursuance of the Company's order.

In like manner they shall not be at liberty to depart thence with their goods obtained in barter, without first returning to the said place, to enter their goods there and to obtain proper clearance, signed by the Governor and Council, and they shall be bound to return to this country, with their ships and yachts, to the place they sailed from, in order to discharge all their freight into the Company's stores, according to the register and clearance to be brought from thence, on pain of forfeiting their ship and goods for the Company's behoof, should they go and break bulk elsewhere, or have any unregistered goods on board.

The Company promises, during the continuance of the present charter and no longer, not to burden the Patroons and Colonists in that country, either with customs, toll, excise, imposts or any other contributions, and after the expiration hereof, at farthest, with no greater duty than is imposed on goods in this country.

The Company shall not take from the service of the Patroons or Colonists, their man servants or maid servants, even though some person should solicit it; nor receive them, much less suffer them to go from their master's service to that of another, during the term of such years as they are bound for; and if any man servant or maid servant run away, or take his freedom contrary to contract, the Company shall, according to its means, cause such to be delivered into the hands of their masters, to be proceeded against according to the circumstances of the case.

From all definitive judgments pronounced by the Courts of the Patroons or Colonists, for an amount exceeding one hundred guilders, or from such as entail infamy, also from all sentences pronounced in matters criminal, on ordinary prosecution, conformable to the custom of this country, an appeal shall lie to the Governor and Council of the Company in New Netherland.

All Patroons, Colonists and inhabitants are allowed free hunting and fishing, both by land and by water, generally in public woods and rivers in the extent of their lands, according to the order to be made thereupon by the Governor and Council; and the Patroons exclusively within the limits of their Colonies, with the clear understanding that the Governor and Council shall not be excluded therefrom.

All Patroons, inhabitants or Colonists are also allowed to send ships along the coast of New Netherland and the countries circumjacent thereunto, to fish for Cod, &c., and to proceed with the catch straight to Italy or other neutral countries, on condition of paying to the Company for duty, in such case, six guilders per last, and on coming here with their freight, it shall be allowable and sufficient to pay the Company the custom dues alone, without conveying, under pretence of this consent, any other goods elsewhere, on pain of arbitrary punishment, it remaining at the pleasure of the Company the custom dues alone, without conveying, under pretence of this consent, any other goods elsewhere, on pain of arbitrary punishment, it remaining at the pleasure of the Company to put a supercargo on board each ship, on such conditions and terms as hereinbefore set forth.

If any Patroons, inhabitants or Colonists happen by their industry, diligence or otherwise to discover any minerals, precious stones, crystals, marbles, pearlfisheries or such like within the limits of their lands, all such Patroons and Colonists shall give one-fifth part of the nett proceeds to the Company, which for this purpose shall have the power to appoint one or more inspectors, at the charge of said mines and pearlfisheries; but any one finding such without their limits, the same shall belong to the Company on paying the discoverer such premium as the merits of the case shall demand.

The Company shall take all Colonists, whether free or bound to service, under their protection, defend them as far as lies in their power with the force which it has there, against all domestic and foreign wars and violence, on condition that the Patroons and Colonists shall, in such case, put themselves in a suitable state of defence for which purpose each male emigrant shall be obliged to provide himself, at his own expense, with a gun or musket of the Company's regular calibre, or a cutlass and side arms.

And no other Religion shall be publicly admitted in New Netherland except the Reformed, as it is at present preached and practiced by public authority in the United Netherlands; and for this purpose the Company shall provide and maintain good and suitable preachers, schoolmasters and comforters of the sick.

The particular Colonies which happen to lie on the respective rivers, bays or islands shall have the privilege (to wit, each river or island for itself) of designating a deputy who shall give the Governor and Council of that country information respecting his Colonie, and promote its interests with the Council; one of which deputies shall be changed every two years, and all the Colonies shall be obliged to communicate to the Governor and Council there a pertinent report at least every twelve months, of their condition and of the lands in their vicinity.

The Company shall exert itself to provide the Patroons and Colonists, on their order, with as many Blacks as possible, without however being further or longer obligated thereto than shall be agreeable.

The Company reserves unto itself all large and small tythes, all waifs, the right of mintage, laying out highways, erecting forts, making war and peace, together with all wildernesses, founding of cities, towns and churches, retaining the supreme authority, sovereignty and supremacy, the interpretation of all obscurity which may arise out of this Grant, with such understanding, however, that nothing herein contained shall alter or diminish what has been granted heretofore to the Patroons in regard to high, middle and low jurisdiction.

The Company shall, accordingly, appoint and keep there a Governor, competent Councillors, Officers and other Ministers of Justice for the protection of the good and the punishment of the wicked; which Governor and Councillors, who are now, or may be hereafter, appointed by the Company, shall take cognizance, in the first instance, of matters appertaining to the freedom, supremacy, domain, finances and rights of the General West India Company; of complaints which any one (whether stranger, neighbor or inhabitant of the aforesaid country) may make in case of privilege, innovation, dissuetude, customs, usages, laws or pedigrees; declare the same corrupt or abolish them as bad, if circumstances so demand; of the cases of minor children, widows, orphans and other unfortunate persons, regarding whom complaint shall first be made to the Council holding prerogative jurisdiction in order to obtain justice there; of all contracts or obligations; of matters pertaining to possession of benefices, fiefs, cases of lease majestatis, of religion and all criminal matters and excesses prescribed and unchallenged, and all persons by prevention may receive acquittance from matters there complained of; and generally take cognizance of, and administer law and justice in, all cases appertaining to the supremacy of the Company.

JOURNAL OF NEW NETHERLAND;
Written in the years 1641, 1642, 1643, 1644, 1645, and 1646

From a Manuscript in the Royal Library at the Hague.

Brief Description of New Netherland.

New Netherland, so called because it was first frequented and peopled by the free Netherlanders, is a province in the most northerly part of America, situate between N. England (which bounds it on the N. E. side) and Virginia, lying to the S. W. Its entire length is washed by the ocean and has a clean sandy beach resembling very much that of Flanders or Holland, having, except the rivers, few bays or harbors for ships. The air is very temperate, inclining to dryness, healthy, little subject to sickness. The four seasons of the year are about as in France or the Netherlands; the difference being, the spring is shorter, because it begins later; the summer is hotter, because it comes on more suddenly; the autumn is long and very pleasant; the winter cold and liable to much snow. Two winds ordinarily prevail, the N. W. in winter, and the S. W. in summer; the other winds are not common; the N. W. corresponds with our N. E., because it blows across the country from the cold point, like our N. E. The S. W. is dry and hot like our S. E., because it comes from the warm countries; the N. E. is cold and wet like our S. W., for similar reasons. The aspect of the country is very like that of France; the land is reasonably high and level, to wit, along the coast, broken by small hills which are rocky and unfit for cultivation; further in the interior are pretty high mountains, exhibiting generally strong indications of minerals; between those mountains flow a great number of small streams; there are even in places, some, but not many, lofty mountains of extraordinary height; in fertility, the country falls behind no province in Europe both as to excellence and cleanness of fruits and seeds. There are three principal rivers, namely: the Fresh, the Mauritius, and the South rivers; all three reasonably wide and deep, adapted to the navigation of large ships twenty-five leagues up, and of common sloops even unto the falls; a canal extends from the river Mauritius to beyond the Fresh river, and forms an island forty leagues in length, called Long Island. This is the ordinary passage from N. England to Virginia, having on both sides many harbors for anchorage, so that people make no difficulty about navigating it in winter. The country is for the most part covered with trees, except a few valleys and some large flats, seven or eight leagues and less in extent; the trees consist as in Europe, of oak, hickory, chestnut, vines. The animals also are of the same species as ours, except lions and some other strange beasts; many bears, abundance of wolves, which harm nothing but small cattle. Elks and deer in vast numbers, foxes, beavers, otters, minx, and such like. The fowls which are natural to the country, are turkeys, like ours, swans, geese of three sorts, ducks, teals, cranes, herons, bitterns; two sorts of partridges, four sorts of heath fowl or pheasants. The river fish is like that of Europe, namely: carp, sturgeon, salmon, pike, perch, roach, eel, etc. In the salt waters are found cod, shellfish, herring, and so forth; also abundance of oysters and muscles.

The Indians are of ordinary stature, strong and broad shouldered; olive color, light and nimble of foot, subtle in disposition, of few words, which they previously well consider; hypocritical, treacherous, vindictive, brave and pertinacious in self defence; in time of need, resolute to die. They seem to despise all the torments that can be inflicted on them, and do not utter a single moan, they go almost naked, except a flap which hangs before their nakedness, and on their shoulders a deer skin, or a mantle, a fathom square, of woven turkey feathers, or of peltries sewed together; they make use now generally of blue or red (duffels), in consequence of the frequent visits of the Christians. In winter they make shoes of deer skin, manufactured after their fashion. Except their chiefs, they have generally but one wife whom they frequently change according to caprice; she must do all the work, plant corn and cut wood, and attend to whatever else is to be done. The Indians are divided into various nations. They differ even in language, which would be altogether too long to be related in this brief space. They dwell together, mostly from friendship, in tribes commanded by a chief, who is the General, and usually called Sackema; he does not possess much authority and but little distinction, unless in their dances and other ceremonies. They have hardly any knowledge of God; no Divine Worship, no law, no justice; the strongest does what he pleases, and the young men are masters. Their weapons are the bow and arrow, in the use of which they are wonderful adepts. Hunting and fishing, in addition to the maize which the women plant, furnish them food.

BY WHOM AND HOW NEW NETHERLAND WAS PEOPLED.

The subjects of the Lords States General, had frequented this country a long time ago, solely for the purpose of the fur trade. Since the year 1623, the Incorporated West India Company caused four forts to be erected, two on the River Mauritius, and one on each of the others; the largest, which their Honors named New Amsterdam, stands on the point formed by the Mauritius and the other river already mentioned; six and thirty miles higher up, is another fort called Orange; that on the south river is named Nassauw, and that on the Fresh river, the Good Hope, in which the Company hath since continually maintained garrisons. In the beginning, their Honors sent thither a certain number of settlers, and caused to be erected at great expense, three saw mills, which never realized any profit of consequence on account of their great charge; a great deal of money was also expended for the advancement of the country, but it never began to be settled until every one was permitted to trade with the Indians, inasmuch as, up to that time, no one calculated to remain there longer than the expiration of his bounden time, and therefore did not apply himself to agriculture; yea, even the Colonie of Renselaerswyck was of little consequence. But as soon as the trade was opened, many servants who had prospered under the Company applied for their discharge, built houses and formed plantations, spread themselves far and wide, each seeking the best land, and to be nearest to the Indians, in order thus to trade with them advantageously; others bought

sloops with which to sell goods at the north and at the south, and as the
Directors gave free passage from Holland thither, that also caused many
to come. On the other hand, the English came both from Virginia and
N. England, on account of the good opportunity to plant tobacco here; first,
divers servants, whose time had expired; afterwards, families, and finally,
entire colonies, having been forced to quit that place, in order to enjoy freedom of conscience, and to escape from the insupportable government of
New England, and because many more commodities were to be obtained
here than there, so that in place of seven bouweries and two @ three plantations which were here, thirty bouweries were to be seen as well cultivated
and stocked as in Europe,   and   one hundred plantations which, in two
or three   years   would become regular bouweries, for after the tobacco
was out of the ground, corn was planted there without ploughing, and the
winter was employed preparing new lands.   The English colonies had settled under us by patent on equal terms with the others.   Each of these was
in appearance not less than one hundred families strong, exclusive of the
Colonie of Rensselaerswyck, which is prospering, with that of Myndert
Meyndertsz and Cornelis Melyn, who began first.   Also the Village of N.
Amsterdam around the fort, one hundred families, so that there was appearance of producing supplies in a year for fourteen thousand souls, without
straightening the country, and had there not been a want of laborers or farm
servants, twice as much could be raised, considering that fifty lasts of rye
and fifty lasts of peas were still remaining around the fort, after a large
quantity had been burnt and destroyed by the Indians, who in a short time
quickly brought this country to nought and had well nigh destroyed this
bright hope, in the manner following.

THE CAUSES AND CONSEQUENCE OF THE NEW NETHERLAND WAR.

We have already stated that the Liberty to trade with the Indians was the cause of the increase of population in N. Netherland. We shall now show that it also is the cause of its ruin; producing two opposite effects, and that not without reason as will appear from what follows.

This Liberty, then, which in every respect was most gratefully received; which should have been used like a precious gift, was very soon perverted to a great abuse. For every one thought that now was the acceptable time to make his fortune; withdrew himself from his fellow, as if deeming him suspected and the enemy of his desire, sought communication with the Indians from whom it appeared his profit was to be derived, all contrary to their High Mightinesses' motto. That created first, a division of power of dangerous consequence; then produced altogether too much familiarity with the Indians, which in a short time brought forth contempt, usually the Father of Hate. For, not satisfied with merely taking them into their houses in the customary manner, they attracted them by extraordinary attention, such as admitting them to Table, laying napkins before them, presenting Wine to them and more of that kind of thing, which they did not receive like Esop's man, but as their due and desert, insomuch that they were not content, but began to hate, when such civilities were not shown them. To this familiarity and freedom succeeded another Evil: as the cattle usually roamed through the woods without a Herdsman, they frequently came among the corn of the Indians which was unfenced on all sides, committing great damage there; this led to frequent complaints on the part of the latter, and, finally, to revenge on the cattle, without sparing even the horses which were valuable in the country. Moreover, many of our's took the Indians into their employ, making use of them in their house work; thus exposing to them our entire circumstances; soon becoming weary of work, the Indians took leg-bail and stole much more than the amount of their wages. This Liberty caused still greater mischief: for the inhabitants of Renselaerswyck, who were as many traders as persons, perceiving that the Mohawks were craving for guns, which some of them had already received from the English, paying for each as many as Twenty Beavers and for a pound of powder as many as Ten to Twelve guilders, came down in greater numbers than usual where guns were plenty, purchasing them at a fair price, realizing in this way considerable profit; they afterwards obtained some from their Patroon for self defence, in time of need, as we suppose. This extraordinary gain was not long kept secret, the traders coming from Holland soon got scent of it, and from time to time brought over great quantities, so that the Mohawks in a short time were seen with fire locks; powder and lead in proportion. Four hundred armed men knew how to make use of their advantage, especially against their enemies,

51

dwelling along the River of Canada, against whom they have now achieved
many profitable forays where before they had but little advantage; this
caused them also to be respected by the surrounding Indians even as far
as the Sea coast, who must generally pay them tribute, whereas, on the contrary, they were formerly obliged to contribute to these. On this account
the Indians endeavored no less to procure Guns, and through the familiarity which existed between them and our people, began to solicit the latter
for Guns and powder, but as such was forbidden on pain of Death, and could
not remain secret in consequence of the general conversation, they could
not be obtained. This, added to the previous contempt, greatly augmented
the hatred which stimulated them to conspire against us, beginning first
with insults which they everywhere -indiscreetly uttered, railing at us as
Materiotty (that is to say) cowards---that we might, indeed be something
on water, but of no account on land, and that we had neither a great Sachem
nor Chiefs. [Here two pages are wanting.]   . . . he of Witqueschreek,
living N. E. of the Island Manhattan, perpetrated another murder in the
house of an old man, a wheelwright, with whom he was acquainted (having
been in his son's service); being well received and suppled with food, and
pretending a desire to buy something, whilst the old man was taking from the
chest the cloth the Indian wanted, the latter took up an axe and cut his head
off; moreover, plundering the house, and then ran away. This outrage obliged the Director to demand satisfaction from the Sachem who refused it,
saying, That he was sorry twenty Christians had not been murdered and that
this Indian had only avenged the death of his Uncle who had been slain over
one and twenty years previously by the Dutch. Whereupon, the Commonalty
were called together by the Director to consider this affair; who all appeared and presently twelve men delegated from among them, answered the pro-
positions, and resolved at once on war, should the murderer be refused;
that the attack should be made in the harvest when the Indians were hunting;
meanwhile, an effort should be again made by kindness to obtain justice,
which was accordingly several times sought for but in vain.

The time being come, many obstacles arose and operations were post-
poned until the year 1642, when it was resolved to avenge the perpetrated
outrage. Thereupon spies looked up the Indians who lay in their village
suspecting nothing, and eighty men were detailed and sent thither under the
command of Ensign Hendrick van Dyck. The guide being come with the
troops in the neighborhood of the Indian wigwams, lost his way in consequence of the darkness of the night. The Ensign became impatient and turned back without having accomplished any thing. The journey, however, was
not without effect, for the Indians, who remarked by the trail made by our
people in marching, that they had narrowly escaped discovery, sued for
peace, which was granted them on condition that they should either deliver
up the murderer or inflict justice themselves. This they promised, but
did not keep their word.

Some weeks after this, Miantenimo, principal Sachem of Sloops Bay,
came here with one hundred men, passing through all the Indian Villages
soliciting them to a general War against both the English and the Dutch,
whereupon some of the neighboring Indians attempted to set our powder on
fire and to poison the Director or to enchant him by their devilry, as their
ill will was afterwards made manifest as well in fact as by report. Those
of Hackingsack, otherwise called Achter Col, had, with their neighbors,

killed an Englishman, a servant of one David Pietersz., and a few days after shot dead, in an equally treacherous manner, a Dutchman who sat roofing a house in the Colonie of Myndert Meyndertz, having settled there against the advice of the Director and the will of the Indians, and had caused, by the continual damage the cattle committed, no little dissatisfaction to the Indians, and contributed greatly to the War. The Commonalty began then to be afraid, and not without reason, having the Indians daily in their houses. The murderers were frequently demanded, either living or dead, even with a promise of reward; a scoffing answer was always returned by the Indians, who laughed at us. Finally, the Commonalty, seriously distrusting the Director, suspecting him of conniving with the Indians, that an attempt was making to sell Christian blood and resolved, that the will of the entire Commonalty was surrendered to him, inasmuch as he would not avenge blood, they would do it, be the consequence what it may. The Director hereupon advised Pacham, the Sachem, who interested himself in this matter, warning him that we would wait no longer, inasmuch as satisfaction had not been given.

Meanwhile God wreaked vengeance on those of Witquescheck without our knowledge through the Mahicanders dwelling below Fort Orange, who slew seventeen of them and made prisoners of many women and children; the remainder fled through a deep snow to the houses of the Christians on and around the Island Manhatens. They were most humanely received, being half dead of cold and hunger, and supported for fourteen days; even some of the Director's corn was sent to them. A short time after, another panic seized the Indians, which caused them to fly to divers places in the vicinity of the Dutch. This opportunity to wreak vengeance for the innocent blood, induced some of the Twelve men to represent to the Director that the time was now come; whereupon, they received for answer, that they should put their request in writing; which was done, by three, in the name of all, in a petition to be allowed to attack those of Hackingsack, lying in two divisions ----on the Manhatens and at Pavonia. This was granted after a protracted discussion, too long to be reported here, so that the design was executed that same night; the Burghers attacked those who lay a short mile from the fort, and the Soldiers those of Pavonia; at which two places about eighty Indians were killed, and thirty were taken prisoners. Next morning, before the return of the troops, a man and woman were shot at Pavoni who had come either through curiosity to look at, or to plunder the dead; the soldiers rescued a young child, which the woman had in her arms.

The Christians residing on Long Island also requested by petition to be allowed to attack and slay the Indians thereabout, which was refused; as these especially had done us no harm and showed us every friendship. (Yea, had even voluntarily killed some of the Raritans, our enemies, hereinbefore mentioned). Yet, notwithstanding, some Christians attempted, secretly with two wagons, to steal maize from these Indians; which, they perceiving, endeavored to prevent; thereupon three Indians were shot dead; two houses standing opposite the fort, were in return forthwith set on fire. The Director knowing nought of this, sent at once some persons to inquire the reason. The Indians showing themselves afar off, called out---Be ye our friends? Ye are mere corn stealers---making them also parties. This induced one of the proprietors of the burnt houses to upbraid, therewith, one Maryn Adriaenzen, who, at his own request, had led the freemen in the attack on the Indians, and who, being reinforced by an English troop, had afterwards undertaken two bootless expeditions in the open field. Imagining that the Director had accused him, being one of the signers of the petition, he determined to revenge himself.

With this resolution he proceeded to the Director's house, armed with a pistol, loaded and cocked, and a hanger by his side; coming unawares into the Director's room, he presents his pistol at him, saying, What devilish lies art thou reporting of me? but by the promptness of one of the bystanders, the shot was prevented, and he arrested. A short time after, Marine's man and another entered the fort, each carrying a loaded gun and pistol---the first fired at the Director, who having had notice, withdrew to his house, the bullets passed into the walls along side the door behind him; the sentinel firing immediately at the fellow who had discharged his gun, brought him down. Shortly afterwards, some of the Commonalty collected before the Director, riotously demanding the prisoner; they were answered, that their request should be presented in order and in writing; which was done by about 25 men, who asked the Director to pardon the criminal. The matter was referred to them to decide conscientiously thereupon; in such wise, that they immediately went forth; without hearing parties or seeing any complaints or documents, they condemn him in a fine of five hundred guilders, and to remain three months away from the Manhattens; but on account of the importance of the affair, and some considerations, it was resolved to send the criminal, with his trial, to Holland, which . . . . .

The winter passed in this confusion, mingled with great terror; the season came for driving out the cattle, which obliged many to desire peace. On the other hand, the Indians seeing also that it was time to plant maize, were not less solicitous for a cessation of hostilities; so after some negotiation, peace was concluded in May, A 1643, rather in consequence of the importunity of some, than of the opinion entertained by others, that it would be durable.

The Indians kept still after this peace, associating daily with our people; yea even the greatest chiefs came to visit the Director. Meanwhile Pacham, a crafty man, ran through all the villages urging the Indians to a general massacre. Thereupon it happened that certain Indians called Wappingers, dwelling sixteen leagues up the river, with whom we never had the least trouble, seized a boat coming from Fort Orange, wherein were only two men, and full four hundred beavers. This great booty stimulated others to follow the example; so that they seized two boats more, intending to overhaul the fourth also; from which they were driven, with loss of six Indians. Nine Christians, including two women, were murdered in these captured barks; one woman and two children remaining prisoners. The rest of the Indians, as soon as their maize was ripe, followed this example; and through semblance of selling beavers, killed an old man and woman, leaving another man with five wounds, who, however, fled to the fort, in a boat, with a little child in his arms, which, in the first outbreak, had lost father and mother, and now grandfather and grandmother; being thus twice rescued, through God's merciful blessing, from the hands of the Indians; first, when two years old. Nothing was now heard but murders; most of which were committed under pretense of coming to put Christians on their guard.

Finally, the Indians took the field and attacked the bouweries at Pavonia. Two ships of war and a privateer, were here at the time, and saved considerable cattle and grain. Probably it was not possible to prevent the destruction of four bouweries on Pavonia, which were burnt; not by open violence, but by stealthily creeping through the bush with fire in hand, and in this way igniting the roofs, which are all either of reed or straw; one covered with plank, was preserved at the time.

The Commonalty were called together, who were sore distressed. They chose Eight, in the stead of the previous Twelve, persons to aid in advising what was best; but occupied as each one was, in taking care of his own, nothing beneficial was adopted at that time; nevertheless, it was resolved that as many Englishmen as were in the country, should be enlisted, who were, indeed, now proposing to depart; the third part of these were to be paid by the Commonalty, who so promised, but the pay did not follow.

Terror increasing all over the land, the Eight men assembled, drew up a proposal in writing wherein they demanded: that delegates should be sent to our English neighbors, at the North, to request an auxiliary force of one hundred and fifty men, for whose pay a bill of Exchange should be given for twenty-five thousand guilders; that N. Netherland should be mortgaged to the English as security for the payment thereof, (one of the most influential among the Eight men had, by letter, enforced by precedents, previously endeavored to persuade the Director to this course; as they had resolved to do a few days before) that the provisions destined for Curacao should be discharged from the vessels and the major part of the men belonging to them detained, and that the ships be sent away thus empty. This was not agreed to, nor deemed expedient by the Director. [Here four pages are wanting.]

An expedition was despatched consisting of ---- soldiers under the command of the Sergeant; XL. Burghers under Jochem Pietersen, their Captain; XXXV. Englishmen under Lieutenant Backster; but to prevent all confusion, Councillor La Montagne was appointed General. Coming to Staten Island, they marched the whole night; the huts were found empty and abandoned by the Indians; they got 5 or 6 hundred skepels of corn and burnt the remainder without accomplishing anything else.

Mayane, a Sachem, residing eight miles N. E. of us, between Greenwich (that lies within our jurisdiction) and Stantford, which is English, a fierce Indian who, alone, dared to attack with bow and arrows, three Christians armed with guns, one of whom he shot dead; was, whilst engaged with the other, killed by the third Christian and his head brought hither. It was then known and understood, for the first time, that he and his Indians had done us much injury, though we never had any difference with him. Understanding further that they lay in their houses very quiet and without suspicion in the neighborhood of the English, it was determined to hunt them up and attack them. One hundred and twenty men were sent thither under the preceding command. The people landed at Greenwich in the evening from three yachts, marched the entire night but could not find the Indians, either because the guide had given warning, or had himself gone astray. Retreat was made to the yachts in order to depart as secretly as possible; passing through Stantford some Englishmen were encountered who offered to lead ours to the place where some Indians were; thereupon four scouts were sent in divers directions to make a discovery, who, on returning, reported that the Indians had some notice of our people from the salute the Englishmen fired, but without any certainty; whereupon five and twenty of the bravest men were at once commanded to proceed thither to the nearest village with great diligence. They made the journey, killing eighteen or twenty Indians, capturing an old man, two women and some children to exchange for ours. The other troops, on reaching the place immediately in the yachts, found the huts empty.

The old Indian, captured above, having promised to lead us to Wetquescheck, which consisted of three Castles, sixty-five men were dispatched under Baxter and Peter Cock, who found them empty, though thirty Indians could have stood against Two Hundred soldiers, inasmuch as the castles were constructed of plank five inches thick, nine feet high, and braced around with thick plank studded with port holes. Our people burnt two, reserving the third for a retreat. Marching 8 or 9 leagues further, they discovered nothing but a few huts, which they could not surprize as they were discovered. They returned, having killed only one or two Indians, taken some women and children prisoners and burnt some corn. Meanwhile, we were advised that Pennewitz, one of the oldest and most experienced Indians in the country, and who, in the first conspiracy, had given the most dangerous counsel, to wit: that they should wait and not attack the Dutch until all suspicion had been lulled, and then divide themselves equally through the houses of the Christians and slaughter all of them in one night; was secretly waging war against us with his tribe who killed some of our people and set fire to the houses. It was, therefore, resolved to send thither a troop of one hundred and twenty men, the Burghers in their Company, the English under Sergeant Major van der Hyl (who, a few days previously, had offered his services and was accepted), the old soldiers under Peter Cock, all commanded by Mr. La Montagne, to proceed hence in three Yachts, land in Scout's Bay on Long Island, march towards Heemstede, where there is an English Colonie dependent on us. Some who had been sent forward in advance, dexterously killed an Indian who was out as a spy. Our force formed themselves into two divisions, Van der Hil with fourteen English towards the smallest, and Eighty men towards the largest village, named Matsepe; both were very successful, killing about one hundred and twenty men; one man of ours remained on the field and three were wounded.

Our forces being returned from this expedition, Captain van der Hil was dispatched to Stantfort to get some information there of the Indians. He reported that the guide who had formerly served us and had gone astray in the night, was now in great danger of his life from the Indians, of whom there were about five hundred together, and offered to lead us there to prove that the former mischance was not his fault. One hundred and thirty men were accordingly dispatched under the aforesaid Gen van der Hil and Ensign Hendrick van Dyck. They embarked in three yachts, landed at Greenwich, where they were obliged to pass the night by reason of the great Snow and Storm; in the morning they marched N. W. up over Stony Hills, over which some were obliged to creep. In the evening, about eight o'clock, they came within a league of the Indians, and inasmuch as they should have arrived too early and had to cross two Rivers, one of two hundred feet wide and three deep, and that the men could not afterwards rest in consequence of the cold, it was determined to remain there until about ten o'clock. Orders having been given as to the mode to be observed in attacking the Indians, the men marched forward towards the huts, which were set up in three rows, street fashion, each Eighty paces in length, in a low recess of the mountain, affording complete shelter from the N. W. wind. The moon was then at the full and threw a strong light against the mountain, so that many winters' days were not clearer than it then was. On arriving, the enemy were found on the alert and on their guard, so that our people determined to charge and surround the huts, sword in hand. The Indians behaved like soldiers, deployed in small bands, so that we had in a short time one dead and twelve wounded. They were likewise so hard pressed that it was impossible for one to escape. In a brief space of time, one hundred and eighty were counted dead outside the houses. Presently none durst come forth, keeping themselves within the houses, discharging arrows through the holes. The General seeing that nothing else was to be done, resolved, with Serjeant Major Van der Hil, to set fire to the huts; whereupon the Indians tried every way to escape, not succeeding in which they returned back to the flames, preferring to perish by fire than to die by our hands. What was most wonderful is, that among this vast collection of Men, Women and Children, not one was heard to cry or to scream. According to the report of the Indians themselves, the number then destroyed exceeded five hundred. Some say, full 700, among whom were also 25 Wappingers, our God having collected together there the greater number of our enemies, to celebrate one of their festivals; no more than eight men in all escaped, of whom even three were severely wounded.

The fight ended, several fires were built in consequence of the great cold; the wounded fifteen in number, were dressed and sentinels having been posted by the General, the troops bivouacked there for the remainder of the night. On the next day, the party set out much refreshed in good order, so as to arrive at Stantfort in the evening. They marched with great courage over that wearisome mountain, God affording extraordinary strength to the wounded some of whom were badly hurt; and came in the afternoon to Stantfort after a march of two days and one night, with little rest. The English received our people in a very friendly manner, affording them every comfort. In two days they reached here. A thanksgiving was proclaimed on their arrival. [The remainder is wanting.]

Report of the Deputies of the States General leading to the Recall of Director Kieft because of his Unjust Treatment of the Indians.

Extract of the Report of Henrick van der Capellen to Ryssell, Viersen, Gerrit van Santen, their High Mightinesses' late Deputies to the Assembly of the West India Company at Amsterdam, holden in October 1644. Exhibited 28th December 1644.

High and Mighty Lords,
 The delegates did, on the 25 /15 October etc.
 We repeatedly brought before the Assembly the complaint which was made to your High Mightinesses respecting the cruel massacre perpetrated on the Indians, so that it may be provided against, and the punishment for blood unlawfully shed, may be warded off this State. And it was finally resolved, that all papers relating to this matter, be placed in the hands of the Board of Accounts (Reken kamer) to extract therefrom, by the next Assembly, what ought to be redressed, as is to be seen, No. 7. It was moreover resolved, to recall the Director in order that he defend himself, and to send back in his stead with a temporary commission, Lubbert van Dinslaken who has been formerly there as fiscal, and who is a favorite with the Indians.
 Minerals of copper, iron and lead have been discovered in those countries, particulars of which are given to this Director, to inform himself thereof, and to send hither the real ore to be tested. A private individual has brought with him copper ore that is very rich, and hath also some silver in it; orders have been given to test and investigate it further.

COMMISSION OF PETER STUYVESANT AS DIRECTOR GENERAL OF NEW NETHERLAND.

From the Commissie-boek of the States General
in the Royal Archives at the Hague.

Commission for Petrus Stuyvesant as Director on the Coast of
New Netherland as well as the Island of Curacao
and the places thereupon depending.

The States General of the United Netherlands to all those to whom these Presents shall come, or who shall hear them read, Health. Be it Known: Whereas We have deemed it advisable for the advancement of the affairs of the General Incorporated West India Company not only to maintain the trade and population on the Coast of New Netherland and the places situate thereabout; also, the Islands Curacao, Buenaire, Aruba and their dependencies, which have hitherto been encouraged thither from this country, but also to make new treaties and alliances with foreign princes and to inflict as much injury as possible on the enemy in his forts and strongholds as well by sea as by land; for which purposes it becomes necessary to appoint a person Director; We, therefore, confiding in the probity and experience of Petrus Stuyvesant, formerly entrusted with Our affairs in, and the government of, the aforesaid Island of Curacao and the places theron depending, We, being well pleased with his services there, have commissioned and appointed, and by these presents do commission and appoint the said Petrus Stuyvesant, Director in the aforesaid countries of New Netherland, and the places thereunto adjoining, together with the aforementioned Islands of Curacao, Beunaire, Aruba, and their dependencies; to administer, with the Council as well now as hereafter appointed with him, the said office of Director, both on water and on land, and in said quality, to attend carefully to the advancement, promotion and preservation of friendship, alliances, trade and commerce; to direct all matters appertaining to traffic and war, and to maintain, in all things there, good order for the service of the United Netherlands and the General West India Company; to establish regularity for the safeguard of the places and forts therein; to administer law and justice as well civil as criminal; and, moreover, to perform all that concerns his office and duties in accordance with the Charter, and the general and particular instructions herewith given, and to be hereafter given him, as a good and faithful Director is bound and obliged, by his oath in Our hands to do; Which done, We, therefore, order and command all other officers, common soldiers, together with the inhabitants and natives residing in the aforesaid places as subjects, and all whom it may concern, to acknowledge, respect and obey the said Petrus Stuyvesant as Our Director in the countries and places of New Netherland, and in the Islands of Curacao, Beunaire, Aruba, and their dependencies, and to afford all help, countenance and assistance in the performance of these things, as We have found the same to be for the advantage of the Company. Done in Our Assembly at the Hague, on the xxviii. July, 1646.

INDIAN DEED OF SALE OF STATEN ISLAND
TO BARON VAN DER CAPELLEN

Albany Records, VIII.

We undersigned Natives of North America, hereditary Proprietors of Staten Island, Sachems of Tasp, Taghkospemo of Tappaan, Temris of Gweghongh, Mattenon of Hespatingh, Waertsen of Hackingsack, Nechtan of Hackingsack, Minqualakyn of Hooghkong, Conincks of Hooghkonck, Nigkanis of Gwegkongh, Mintamessems of Gwegkongh, Acchipoor of Hoogkong, declare and certify for ourselves and our posterity, in the presence of the undersigned witnesses, that we transport; first all our Right and property, without any reserve for ourselves or our posterity, forever, to Lubbertus van Dincklage, as agent of the Baron Hendrick van der Capellen, Lord of Ryssel, the whole of Staten Island, called by us Eghquaous, for the following specified goods, to be imported here from England, and to be delivered to us, the original proprietors:---Ten cargoes of shirts; thirty pairs of Ferouse stockings; ten guns; ten staves of lead; thirty lbs. of powder; thirty ells red Dozyn's cloth; two pieces of frieze; thirty kettles, large and small; fifty axes, small and large; twenty-five chisels; a few awls; a few knives.

We engage ourselves to ally with and assist our Friends, if any other savages might insult, molest or assail the inhabitants of Staten Island. In truth whereof, we, the original proprietors, signed this Acte, with the witnesses, with submission to the Courts of Justice at Hospating near Hackingsack on Waerkimins Connie in New Netherland, on the 10th of July, 1657.

TREATY OF PEACE , CONCLUDED WITH
THE ESOPUS INDIANS ON THE 15TH JULY 1660.

Articles of peace, made at the request of the below named chiefs of the savages between the Hon. Petrus Stuyvesant, Director-General of New Netherland and the Sachems or chiefs of the Indians of the Esopus.

Names of the chiefs, who asked for peace in the name of the Esopus savages and in whose presence the peace was concluded:

1.

All hostilities on either side shall cease and all acts and injuries shall be forgotten and forgiven by either side.

Of the Maquas:
Adoghginoakque
Wohesaquade
Oghnecott

2.

The Esopus savages promise to convey, as indemnification, to the aforesaid Director-General all the territory of the Esopus and to remove to a distance from there, without ever returning again to plant.

Of the Mohicans:
Eskuyas, alias Aepje
Ampumet
Catskil:
Keseway
Machaknemeno

3.

They promise further to pay to the said Director-General in return for the ransom, taken for the captured Christians, 500 schepels of Indian corn, one half during the next fall, when the corn is ripe, the other half or its value during the fall next following.

Minquas:

Onderishochque
Kakongeritsschage

Wappings:
Isschachga
Wisachganioe

Of Hackinkesacky:

4.

The Esopus savages promise to keep this treaty inviolable, not to kill horses, cattle, hogs nor even a chicken or if it should happen to be done, then the chiefs undertake to pay for it and in case of refusal one of them shall be kept in prison or under arrest until the loss has been paid or made good, while on the other side the Director-General promises, that the Dutch neither shall be permitted to do any harm to them.

Oratamy
Carstangh
Of Staten-Island
Warrhan

5.

If the Dutch should kill a savage or the savages a Dutchman, war shall not be immediately commenced again for that reason, but a complaint shall be made and the murderers shall be delivered to be punished, as they deserve.

61

The following are the
names of the Esopus
Sachems, with whom
the treaty was made.
Koelcop
Seewackemamo
Neskahewan
Paniyruways

6.

The Esopus savages shall not come armed to the Dutch plantations, houses and habitations, but without arms they may go, come and trade as before.

7.

Whereas the last war was caused by drunken people, no savage shall be allowed to drink brandy or strong liquor in or near the Dutch plantations, houses or settlements, but he must go with it to his land or to some distant place in the woods.

8.

Included in this peace shall be all, not only the aforementioned tribes of savages, but also all others, who are in friendship with the Director-General, among others especially the chief of Long-Island, Tapousagh and all his savages; if any act of hostility should be committed against these, the Director-General would consider it his duty, to assist them.

9.

The aforesaid chiefs, as mediators and advocates of the Esopus tribe, remain bondsmen and engage themselves, to have this treaty kept inviolate and in case the Esopus Indians should break the peace, now concluded, they undertake altogether to assist the Dutch to subdue the Esopus savages.

10.

On the foregoing conditions the said Director-General offered first to the aforesaid mediators and they accepted each a piece of cloth and to the chiefs of the Esopus savages 3 of their captives and each a piece of cloth.

Thus done and concluded at the settlement on the Esopus, under the blue sky, in presence of the Hon. Marten Cregier, Burgomaster of the City of Amsterdam in New-Netherland, Oloff Stevenson Cortland, ex-Burgomaster, Arent van Curler, deputy of the Colony of Renselaerswyck and many people of the Esopus, both Christians and Indians, the 15th July 1660.

P. Stuyvesant   Marten Cregier
Oloff Stevenson   A. van Curler.

Endorsements on the foregoing:

5th of August.

After the report of the Hon. Director-General Petrus Stuyvesant, concerning the occurrences at (the Esopus), had been heard and read in Council, the same was duly thanked, on the day as above.

The peace at the Esopus having been concluded, the Director-General and his party left for Fort Orange and what has passed there, worth writing down, has been recorded hereafter. This pro memoria.

JACOB STEENDAM'S VERSES
COMPOSED FOR PLOCKHOY'S PAMPHLET
ENCOURAGING IMMIGRATION TO HIS COLONY
ON THE DELAWARE (1662)

You poor, who know not how your living to obtain;
You affluent, who seek in mind to be content;
Choose you New Netherland, which no one shall disdain;
Before your time and strength here fruitlessly are spent.

The birds obscure the sky, so numerous in their flight;
The animals roam wild, and flatten down the ground;
The fish swarm in the waters and exclude the light;
The oysters there, than which none better can be found,
Are piled up, heap on heap, till islands they attain;
And vegetation clothes the forest, mean and plain.

. . . a living view does always meet your eye,
Of Eden, and the promised land of Jacob's seed;
Who would not, then, in such a formed community,
Desire to be a Freeman; and the rights decreed,
To each and every one, by Amstel's burgher lords,
T'enjoy?   and treat with honor what their rule awards?

                                                  (Murphy's translation)

APPEAL TO THE FAITHFUL IN THE UNITED STATES
OF NORTH AMERICA MAY 25, 1846

(This translation of Antonie Brummelkamp's and Albertus C. Van Raalte's appeal appeared in the Christian Intelligencer of October 15, 1846, with a short introduction by the Rev. Thomas de Witt (1791-1874), minister of the Collegiate Reformed Church in New York.)

The following is a translation of the "Appeal to the Faithful in America" issued by Rev. Messrs. Brummelkamp and Van Raalte, in behalf of the Christian brethren who have Separated from the Established Reformed Church, who purpose emigrating to America, which I promised last week. I have been spared the trouble of translating it myself as I have just received this translation from the pen of Mrs. S., a member of Dr. Isaac Wyckoff's church in Albany, who emigrated from Holland a short time since. A view of the history of the Secession, and of its present state, will be given hereafter, in the course of reminiscences of the Fatherland, to be published in your columns.

Thomas De Witt.

To the Faithful in the United States of North America:
Beloved brethren and sisters in the Mediator between God and man, the Lord Jesus Christ the Son both of God and Man, who is over all, God blessed for ever; who with us, though by nature dead in trespasses and sins, by the riches of God's mercy, are born again into a living hope, by faith in God's Son, our crucified, but also risen and sitting at the right hand of God, and now expected, according to the working of His mighty power, whereby He will be glorified in us who believe - grace be to you, and peace from God our Father and from the Lord Jesus Christ by the Holy Spirit.

Brethren and sisters, though separated from you by the ocean, we have a word to you. We, by the great mercy of God our Saviour, ministers of God's word, servants of the blood-bought Church of God, ask for the exercise of the communion of saints, and call upon your compassion towards many of the Lord's children, towards many poor and needy of your fellowmen.

But that you may be able to grant us some confidence, we will endeavor to make you better acquainted with our persons, circumstances, and purposes.

After having completed our studies at the University at Leiden, more than ten years since, we entered into the ministry of the Word, and being partakers of the true and living faith, and through God's Spirit partaking a revival of His children, we soon found ourselves standing in opposition to our national, or world-church, which in many instances is nothing but a mere State machine, dependent upon worldly government, and supported by the State fund, with a minister of public worship at its head. Because we rather choose to obey the Word of God, than the despotic rules and regulations of their Church government, which estranges itself more and more from God's truth, we, together with some more ministers, were troubled and hindered in the ministry of the Word. The consequences of this were that amidst much reviling and persecution, viz., fining, quartering, and imprisonment -   for in this country it is not permitted to preach the gospel to more than twenty persons at one time - the preaching of the gospel also is made dependent from its being acknowledged by the government as a distinct religious body in the community, and it is limited within buildings appropriated for that purpose by such bodies   - these have formed themselves in every part of the Netherlands small congregations, entirely independent from the government-congregations small and poor according to the world, but, for the most part, out of the middle class of citizens, and consisting in the whole of members who know and feel their forlorn and condemnable condition before God, who take refuge only in the blood of reconciliation, and who desire nothing better but to live during the time of their indwelling in the flesh, according to the will of God, that they may be a sweet savor of Christ, to the praise of God the Father.

Since two years we were ministering to those congregations, lowly and soberly, according to the outward appearance, as many of the vital concerns of those congregations are greatly suffering from the social oppression; for though our members are bound to pay, together with all the other inhabitants, their equal share in the taxes which are imposed upon the public for the support of the church of the land, and of the superstition, yet, not being willing to sacrifice the liberty of our congregation, we judiciously would refuse to accept any subsidies of the land's treasury, if ever such would be offered to us - but we have no fear at all that we shall be brought into the temptation, having been compelled, as we are - in order to get our civil acnowledgement in the community, and through it, the liberty of preaching in church buildings - to promise never to claim any support of the public fund, neither for our churches nor poor. In consequence of this, the cares of the churches, parsonages, for the support of the widows and the poor for ministers and the means of the faithful are rather small, while many, and especially among the more wealthy children of God, are yet lingering behind in the Established Church. This languishing and outward wretched condition of many of our members, and thousands of our fellow-citizens - which stands near related to the deplorable material state of this country, occasioned by the superabundance of its population, and the consequently mutual pressing - the poor, decaying condition of trade and handicraft - the diminution of wages - the invasion of rights of conscience - and finally the quite exhausting tributes or taxes which are daily required to balance our enormous State's debt - by all this we see that our middle class disappears, the wealth of the wealthy increases, and the laboring classes, often, notwithstanding their best efforts, are quite unable, according to the expressed will of God, "that every man should work that he might eat", to get any kind of fixed and sufficient employment by which to make their scanty living, much less to provide for their houses, and to lay something aside in behalf of the widow and fatherless, and the promotion of God's kingdom upon earth. These sad realities have, for some time past, urged us to look for some other part of our globe, as an habitation for many of our Christian countrymen, especially for many of those of our Christian fellow-citizens. In consequence of their inactive and impoverished condition, they find themselves, with their children, reduced to rest embarrassment, if not to the practice of some of these the conscience-defiling traffics, and seek resort to a country where the work awaits the man, and not man the work - where there is no such super-abundance of population as to occasion mutual and continual repulsing, but where God's beautiful creation is still ready to receive men. The more we are forced to look out for such a new habitation, in consequence of the utter failure of all our efforts, during several of the past years, to find employment and livelihood for the multitude of the destitute - and we feel ourselves, moreover, bound to do so, as it is our conviction that idleness or inactivity, not less than slavish labor, usually begets stifling cares, or becomes the exciter of man's inward corruption, the great source of so many deplorable sins, by which our own spiritual interests are endangered, and the general concerns of God's kingdom slighted and injured; by which matrimony is avoided, licentionsness cherished, our offspring neglected, and a stream of social and civil pollution is flowing in the midst of us; by which sin to the one becomes a trifle, and to the other, is a cause that he passes his days sighing and with a spotted conscience.

Though they see more and more in this country the necessity of emigration, yet the nobility are mightily opposed to it, on account of the general loss which they expect from it, at least in case the way does not lead to one of the Dutch owned colonies, for which colonies our Christian people are sorely afraid, as much in consequence of the unhealthy climate, as on account of the oppressive couse of the Dutch government, in relation to religious liberty. For all these reasons we have turned our eyes towards the United States of North America. Our heart's desire and prayer to God is, that on one of those uninhabited regions there may be a spot where our people, by the culture of the ground   for it is this quiet mode of life we prefer above all, and the greatest part of the emigrants are either husbandmen or industrious mechanics   , may find their temporal subsistence secured, and be able also to save their families from the miseries of a declining state of community. Especially we would desire, that they, settling in the same villages and neighborhoods, may enjoy the privilege of seeing their little ones educated in a Christian school - a privilege of which we are here entirely deprived, as the instruction given in the state's schools may be called but a mere general moral one, offensive to neither Jew nor Roman Catholic, and the free schools are quite interdicted. We neither may nor wish to endure this privation any longer. Furthermore, it is our desire to take an active part in the promulgation of God's truth among the heathen, as here with many, by the lack of power, there arises the lack of will. To our great satisfaction, we have heard that in the interior of America, together with all the privileges of religious and scholastic liberty, there is still a great abundance of fertile ground and profitable labor to be found. But as there is not much fund to be expected by mechanics nor either by husbandmen, we are not able to defray all the necessary expenses, neither can we look to defray all the necessary expenses, neither can we look for aid to any of the wealthy of our countrymen, for the above-mentioned reasons. Though a bright and free path of rescue for so many sorely afflicted and godly families is indeed brought within our view, yet still it remains rather inaccessible, at least we have already been obliged to send away many entreating, godly, needy, miserable fellow-creatures, to see them sink still deeper in want and destitution. God commands us that we must love our neighbor not in words only, but in deed and truth; that whatsoever our hand finds to do, we should do it with all our might; it is in accordance with those principles that we boldly apply to you, beloved brethren and sisters, beseeching you to grant us your aid and assistance in this precious work, to rescue many members of the body of Christ - many fellow creatures from a really great distress, which, by the present condition of the land, threatens to become more distressing still, and more pernicious for the welfare of the rising generation. We entreat you to aid and assist us with your counsel, with your wealth, and with whatsoever the Lord our God has entrusted to you. Such we beseech of you with perfect boldness, assured as we are, that it shall work together for your salvation, and that your good works shall be rich in fruits of thanksgiving unto God. We ask it confidently, not presuming that either your hearts or hands, by any prejudice, will be fenced against a Dutch colony on North America's ground, as also this work is to our hearts a very dear and precious task. Once more, dearly beloved brethren and sisters O! do assist us, that we may become mutually acquainted in God, through Christ, in performing good works, that we may together rejoice in these new and sweet bonds of Christian love and charity.

The following has already taken place here. Besides a few single families and persons who removed previously, there left in the autumn of last year a company of about thirty persons, out of our neighborhood and elsewhere, all respectable citizens and husbandmen. Their destination was to Macrean, or Decator, in Vandalia, State of Illinois. We hope they have succeeded in finding a livelihood. Then a small Society has been formed, with the purpose of promoting emigration - to prevent as much as possible the separation of the emigrants from one another, and to secure, by their remaining united, the interests both of religion and education of the young. By means of funds furnished by this Society, those families of clever, industrious mechanics, Christian people, who, with fear and trembling, were anticipating the winter season, have been enabled to make their way to one of the seaports of America, there to make, by industry and economy, provisions for their remaining parents and friends, in aiding them to liquidate their affairs in the native land, as also to procure them the means of going thither among their Dutch Christian countrymen. At this moment a number of no less than forty Christian persons, for the most part farmers, are quitting the land of their nativity, and it is especially those whom we would recommend to you, to aid them with your counsel. They would make their journey either over the lakes or along the Ohio to Milwaukee in Wisconsin, to the Dutch Christians settled there. Let them know which way or mode of travelling is the most secure and with the least expense for those of our people who may follow. This will be as much as the Lord will enable us to help along with their most necessary expenses. May it please the Lord to move in the hearts of the godly in the United States, the bowels of their compassion that they may confirm the hope and the prospects of many distressed and faithful Christians in the Netherlands, of rescue out of so many anxious cares, to the praise of God in Christ Jesus. We beseech you, therefore, do come to our aid! Though we feel that your shoulders are, probably, laden with many burdens and calls for charity, yet, in the other hand, we are sure that the Christians in America are graciously spared from that distressful decline in business, and also from those heavy taxes or duties under which our people are bowed down. Moreover we know that union makes power and that in the kingdom of God the penny of the poor widow is of great importance.

If you should think it judicious to circulate, by means of some of your American papers, this our petition among the faithful, scattered throughout the states, you would greatly oblige us, being confident that, by the goodness of God, the voice of prayer shall, for his Son's sake, come, here and there, to the hearts of his people. In the full conviction that the kingdom of God does not consist in word, but in power - that we ought to love one another in deed and in truth - that we have to bear each other's burdens - that the commandments of God not only may, but must be attended to, cost what it will, and that we therefore are not permitted to separate the injunction to work and to eat - that every Christian is in duty bound to provide for his house, wherever such may be; yea, more, that he ought to be enabled to visit the widow and the fatherless in their affliction, and to serve the kingdom of the Lord of his substance-that he ought to keep himself undefiled before the world - that he is not to bring up his children in a mere general moral way, but in the nurture and admonition of the Lord - and being assured, moreover, that though we are surrounded with manifold distressing obscurities, and often go astray, yet, that we desire above all things to serve the Lord all the time of our lives - we lay this our petition before you, and humbly recommend it to the Lord who reigneth and dwelleth in in the hearts of the children of men.

We close with the supplication of our hearts, that the God and Father of our Lord Jesus Christ, the God of our salvation, by His almighty power and the riches of His mercy, may make both you and ourselves diligent and abounding in obedience; and that the great unspeakable truth, that we have in God, for all eternity, a reconciled God and Father in Christ, who has thrown all our sins behind his back, and who never more shall be angry with us - may be to our souls the sweet source of comfort and happiness - that the hope of life may enable us to go on our ways rejoicing, and that we, having our hearts burning with love, carry forth in ourselves the image of God, and live to be a blessing upon the earth.

Your most appreciable and well-wishing brethren in Christ.

A.C. van Raalte, V. D. M.
A. Brummelkamp, V. D. M.

Arnhem, June 1846

PASSENGER LIST OF THE "SOUTHERNER,"
ROTTERDAM TO NEW YORK, SEPT.24 - NOV.17, 1846

"Report and List of the Passengers on board of the bark Southerner of Boston whereof Tully Crosby is master, burthen two hundred seventy-six tons and 65/95th of a ton, bound from the Port of Rotterdam for New York:

Steerage Passengers

1. Jan Slotboom, 27, male, blacksmith
2. W. P. Slotboom, 29, female
3. Wilhelm B. Slotboom, 3 1/2, male, son
4. Johan Slotboom, 2, male, son
5. S. C. Slotboom, 8 months old, daughter
6. Frans Smit, 44, male, blacksmith
7. Gesina Smit, 36, female
8. Geerardus Smit, 12, male, son
9. Dina Smit, 10, female, daughter
10. Mina Smit, 7, female, daughter
11. Jacobus Smit, 5, male, son
12. Francina Smit, 3, female, daughter
13. George H. Smit, 8 months old infant son
14. Wouter Van den Brink, 36, male, car-carpenter
15. Geertje Van der Sande, 50 female
16. Chrisje Van den Brink, 18, female
17. Wouter Van der Sande, 60, male, farmer
18. Leentje Botsen, 30, female
19. Theod. Botsen, 30, male, farmer
20. P. Botsen, 1, male, son
21. F. A. B. Caspers, 30, male, painter
22. Rosalie Theresia Briedie, 22, female
23. Henriette Josep. Caspers, 11 months, daughter
24. P. C. Olivier, 49, male, machinist
25. E. G. Olivier, 23, male, copper-worker
26. Amelia H. Van Supkamp, 36, female
27. W. DeGroot, 42, male, farmer
28. Albert P. Olivier, 5 months, son
29. Louisa Amelia Olivier, 2 months, daughter
30. Maarten Klaasen, 36, male, laborer
31. Jan Korten, 40, male, laborer
32. Geesje Klaasen, 45, female
33. Antonie Korten, 10, male, son
34. Janna Korten, 7, female, daughter
35. Gerrit Korten, 4, male, son
36. Evert Klaasen, 33, male, farmer
38. Hendrik Jan Claasen, 4, male, son
39. Aaltje Klaasen, 11 months, daughter
40. Egbert Dunnewind, 53, male farmer
41. Tennigse Dunnewind, 19, female
42. Hendrik Dunnewind, 13, male
43. Gerrit Dunnewind, 9, male
44. Evert Dunnewind, 8, male
45. Harm Kok, 50, male, farmer
46. Janna Dunnewind, 47, female
47. Hermine Kok, 20, female, daughter
48. Jan Kok, 19, male, son
49. Hendrik Kok, 15, male, son

50. Albert Kok, 11, male, son
51. Martin Kok, 11, male, son
52. Jan Harm Kok, 4, male, son
53. H. Jan Kok, 1, male, son
54. Bernardus Grootenhuis, 32, male
    painter
55. Janna Hogewind, 27, female
56. Johannes Grootenhuis, 5, male, son
57. Jacobus Grootenhuis, 10 months,
    son
58. Hendrik Oldemeijer, 40, male,
    farmer
59. Dina Schepers, 40, female
60. Jan Oldemeijer, 7, male, son
61. Hermanus Lankheet, 31, male,
    miller
62. Samuel Korman, 26, male,
    carpenter
63. Roelofje Beutem, 24, female
64. Mayaline Korman, 7 months, daugh-
    ter
65. Dirk Plasman, 48, male, farmer
66. Aaltje Plasman, 46, female
67. Willem Plasman, 18, male, son
68. Frederik Plasman, 11, male, son
69. Jannigje Plasman, 8, male, son
70. Widow Van Zee, 34, female
71. Mina Van Zee, 34, female
72. Sophia G. Van Zee, 32, female
73. Jan H. Epping Van Zee, 30, male,
    blacksmith
74. Johanna Van Zee, 26, female
75. Lubbertus Van Zee, 26, male, baker
76. Jan Willem Van Zee, 24, male,
    baker
77. Willem Notting, 35, male, farmer
78. M. Notting, 26, female
79. Hendrik Notting, 1, male, son
80. Widow Laarman, 60, fe-
    male

81. Jan Laarman, 30, male,
    farmer
82. Geesje Laarman, 25, fe-
    male
83. Jan Hendrik Laarman,
    1 1/2, male, son
84. Albert Notting, 11, male,
    son
85. Evert Zagers, 32, male,
    weaver
86. Roelofje Vrielink, 40, male
87. Hendrik Zagers, 5, male
88. Egbert Frederiks, 31, male
    laborer
89.
90. Roelofje Frederiks, 2, fe-
    male, daughter
91. Geesje Frederiks, 9 weeks
    infant, daughter
92. J. Van den Boogaard, 28,
    male, tailor
93. Maria Van den Boogaard,
    30, female
94. Lena Van den Boogaard, 3,
    female, daughter
95. Elizabeth Van den Boo-
    gaard, 11 months, infant
    female
96. Casper Schneider, 25, male
    workman
97. T. Van Esterick, 39, male,
    painter
98. G. Blom, 39, male, tailor
99. H. De Kruyf, 29, male,
    tailor
100. Bernard Ebberling, 22,
     wooden shoemaker
101. B. J. Westerhoudt, 33, male
     merchant
102. Aartje Korsman, 21, fe-
     male, servant

Cabin Passengers

103. A. C. Van Raalte, 35, male clergyman
104. Johanna Christina Van Raalte, 32, female
105. Albertus Christiaan Van Raalte, 9 months, son
106. Johanna Maria Van Raalte, 7, female, daughter
107. Benjamin Van Raalte, 5, male, son
108. Dirk Van Raalte, 2, male, son
109. Christina Catherina Van Raalte, 5 months, female
110. Tennegje Lasker, 40, female, servant

"Note: Died, no. 86, Oct. 16, inflammation of bowels; no. 90, Nov. 1, dropsy, sick 12 months; no. 95, Oct. 13, sick when we left port. No. 101 left ship at Rotterdam on eve of sailing."

REPORT OF VISIT TO THE HOLLAND COLONIES (1850)

(The Board of Domestic Missions of the Reformed Church asked the Rev. Isaac N. Wyckoff to visit the Dutch settlements in Michigan and Wisconsin in 1849. His report on what he found led to the union of the immigrant churches with the Reformed Church in America and is therefore one of the most important documents in the history of Dutch immigration).

The undersigned begs leave respectfully to report the fulfillment of his mission, to the Board of Domestic Missions of the Reformed Protestant Dutch Church of North America.

Agreeably to your wishes and instructions after I had fulfilled the objects of my delegation to the Rev. the General Assembly of the Presbyterian Church convened at Pittsburg, I went on my way to the Holland Colony. I would first of all gratefully acknowledge the goodness of God and the kindness of Christian men in all my journey. Not a day has my health been in any wise impaired - not a day have I been hindered by stress of weather from prosecuting my mission. Everywhere the kindest personal attentions, and the best facilities for travelling have been offered by the Christian brethern. My journey was made from Pittsburgh by public conveyance through Beaver Canal, and by stage to Cleveland, by steamboat to Detroit, by railroad to Kalamazoo, by mail wagon to Allegan, and then by the voluntary and gratuitous favor of Judge John R. Kellogg's team and man, to the Colony. Such interest as Judge Kellogg a New Englander and his family have shown to our Holland brethern, ought to be recorded here. He hospitably entertained Mrs. A. C. van Raalte and children for three months while a house was erecting in the wilds of the Colony for her reception. He has several times given up his kitchen, and other parts of his dwelling, and the whole of another house he owns to accommodate the Hollanders as they were going through. He has preserved and defended the emigrants from imposition and oppression, and stood by them, as they gratefully express it, met raad en daad "counsel and deed" in all their difficulties.

He traveled with the Rev. A. C. van Raalte to examine lands and greatly contributed to the selection of the glorious country which the Colony now occupies. The Dutch Church thanks him, and may God bless him and his for such kindness!

It was a novel ride and not without peril, from Allegan to the Colony. With a noble span of horses and a wagon made for the purpose we hardly reached the place in eleven hours "with whole bones". How then must the colonists have struggled with ox teams and such wagons as they could get to reach the place.

My reception, as your messenger, by the Colony was almost literally with a shout of joy. There had been sorrow in the colony over many things and not least over the fact that the Dutch Church which they had hoped would have reached the poor emigrants, flying in poverty from persecution, with sympathizing hearts and open arms had seemed to take almost no interest at all in them. With the exception of a few individual brethren, they mourned that the Dutch Church counted them strangers, and had no word of encouragement, no hand of help for them. The reaction, therefore, was electrical. To think that we at last felt for them [cared for them, were willing to help them though late] shot through every heart, and there were many thanksgivings to God for His work of love, and many benedictions on the head of your representative. "Out of their deep poverty" shone "the riches of their liberality" to your commissioner. They feasted us with all they had---but it was mainly a change in pickled port and fine potatoes. But they begin to have butter and eggs and when time permits they can get fine fish out of the lake.

It did not enter into my commission to examine their physical circumstances, and yet I doubt not that both you and many others will be pleased to know some particulars of their locality, progress of settlement, and condition; and I am happy to be able to satisfy so just a curiosity in a way that will gratify every benevolent heart. I arrived on Thursday evening June 1st [really, on May 31]. My plan was to assemble the ministers on Saturday [June 2], make your overtures, and be ready to start for Wisconsin on Monday [June 4]. But brother Van Raalte could not consent to so early a departure. First, the ministerial brethren could not be assembled till Monday, for expresses had to be sent for all. And second, I must see every settlement in order to give a fair account. The appeal was so earnest and reasonable that I consented to remain. On Friday [June 1,] then, I visited the city of Holland. On Saturday [June 2], I walked from morning to night along Indian trails from one clearing and settlement to another in the vicinity. On Monday [June 4 the Classis met. On Tuesday mounted on the doctor's horse the only horse in the colony without a saddle, and Dominie van Raalte and others walking and leading the way, we went forth to visit the several country churches, swam the Black River, halted at Groningen, the nearest province, proceeded on a trail to Zeeland, spent the night with Rev. Cornelius van [der] Meulen's congregation. Wednesday, started early, went by the church of Drenthe, where we dined on butter and bread and coffee, and started for Vriesland, but got lost in our way, and had to employ a good woman as our guide. We at last found Rev. Maarten Anne Ypma, and after looking over his province and being hospitably entertained, and spending the night with him, we returned through the rain next morning to the city.

In my route I gathered the following statistics: The city with its environs contains 235 houses: Groningen, 30; Zeeland, 175; Drenthe, 45; Vriesland, 69; Overyssel, 35; Graafschap, 50. In all about 630 houses, which, at an average of five souls to a house will make the population over 3,000 souls. Some of the farms have two acres chopped and cleared, others five, and so on up to eighty; so that it may be fairly estimated that there are now three thousand acres cut and in progress of clearing.

The face of the country, which I had supposed was very flat, is pleasantly diversified with hill and valley, lake, and stream. The streams are fed by large cranberry marshes, which being themselves supplied by springs, send forth clear and healthy waters. I saw no lands which cannot be easily drained, so as to make them excellent for hay culture. It is a remarkable provision of nature that along the several rivers of Michigan there are broad tracts of natural meadow, affording abundance of pasture for summer and hay for winter. If the character of the forest is a proper index of the quality of the land on which it grows, then the soil is of the most fruitful kind. The trees are wonderful to a dweller on the Hudson. Many and many an oak have I seen from two to three feet in diameter, straight as an arrow, and having from nine to twelve post-cuts of eight feet each, before you reach the limbs. There are thousands of white pines that will yield from two to three thousand feet of clear inch boarding. I measured the stump of an oak five and a half feet in diameter. Three men [I being one] could only touch the tips of our fingers around an ancient sycamore. The most beautiful sugar maples grow on the heavy soils. Black walnut and curled and birds' eye maple and wild cherry trees, all of great dimensions, are plenty, and in many parts hemlocks of the most stately proportions. Whereever the land is sufficiently cultivated, the wheat is splendid, rank in growth and rich in color. Potatoes and turnips of the best quality will be abundant this year, and probably also Indian corn. The prospects of agriculture are full of hope and promise. The heart of the people rejoices amidst all their provisions, in the mercy of God, which has given them such a goodly land and such great progress.

A most cheering fact further encourages the people. It was anticipated from the dark color of the water in the river and lake indicating that it drained a soil deeply filled with vegetable matter, or flowing from much swamps of great depth, that the location would be unhealthy. In the first year that dark anticipation seemed to be considerably realized, for not a few sickened and some died. But just as soon as the people became properly housed, this fear entirely subsided, for directly the colonists enjoyed an unusual average of health. During my whole visit I did not see or hear of a sick person, and this fact is the more conclusive, as this has been uncommonly wet and all the lower grounds have more or less surface water upon them. The early sickness was evidently owing not to badness of climate and air but to exposure to the inclemency of the elements and want of nourishing food.

I ought perhaps to mention in this connection that the Colony has uncommon natural advantages. There is a water power on the Black River driving two sawmills, to which a gristmill will soon be added, and at other points shingle and lath factories, and whatever else requires water power may be added. And there is scarcely on the face of the whole earth a more beautiful harbor for all manner of vessels than the Black Lake. It is about five miles long and varies from a quarter to a mile and a half broad and has a depth varying from seven feet within twenty feet of the city strand, to twenty, thirty, fifty, and even eighty feet. Like all the rivers on the eastern shore, its outlet is obstructed by the sandbars of the Michigan, but let a channel and haven once be formed, and it is the general opinion of all disinterested persons it will be the most desirable harbor and wintering place on all the western side of the peninsula.

For one thousand dollars a pier and plank road of five hundred and sixty yards can be constructed, which will immediately increase the trade ten or one hundred fold. A corps of engineers of the general government is now on the lake making an exact topographical survey of the lake and waters of the Michigan at its mouth. Colonel John R. Bowes, the experienced and gentlemanly leader of the corps, spoke in the highest terms of the beauty and facilities of the lake and harbor.

An enterprising gentleman has just finished and set in operation a steam sawmill that draws up its logs out of the lake and is doing a good business. A company have constructed a wind sawmill which operates well and is capable with an ordinary wind of driving six saws. A tannery is in progress of erection, which will find inexhaustible quantities of quercitron and hemlock bark in the neighborhood; and within the limits of the city is a shipyard, which will be prepared to build all kinds of craft, and the live oak for the hulks and for plank, and the magnificent pines for masts and spars, are in sight on the shores of the lake.

From this description of the physical circumstances of the colony I will turn to the direct object of your commission, which was to inquire into the religious and ecclesiastical relations of this people, to express to them the sympathy of our church, to make an overture for church relation and to offer such aid in their straitness as might be necessary and desirable. To obtain this information Rev. van Raalte deemed it would be expedient to assemble the ministers and the elders of the churches. Accordingly he dispatched letters and messengers to the several ministers and consistories inviting them to a conference with me on Monday June 5th. Quite a large company attended and having opened the conference with prayer and a psalm we spent nearly the whole day in giving and receiving information and comparing ideas. From the assembled brethren I obtained the following facts and statistics. There are seven congregations and four ministers tacitly constituting the Classis of Holland.

			Families	Communicants
1	Church of Holland	Van Raalte	225	250
2	Zeeland	Van der Meulen	175	225
3	Friesland	Ypma	69	125
4	Overyssel	Bolks	35	80
5	Graafschap	Has called Rev. Mr. H. G. Klyn who is on his way to to America	50	100
6	Drenthe	Has made a call but without success	45	79
7	Groningen	Has as yet made no call	30	63

Five of these congregations have erected houses of worship, that of Zeeland is 45 by 60 feet, built of handsomely squared cedar logs with a cupola and bell, and is quite an ornamental building. The Holland house was first built and was more hastily and less neatly constructed. The others are comfortable log houses.

Of all these communicants in these churches it may be said they are praying and hopefully converted person. Their religious habits are very strict and devout. They do all things with prayer and praise. They sing and pray in the morning, after their dinner, and after their supper. They pray when they meet for business. At a bee [or meeting for common work] they pray. The common council of the city opens its sittings with prayer. The appearance and tone of piety is purer and higher than any thing I have ever seen and seemed like the primitive Christians and most beautiful.

The colony is paying as much attention as possible to schools and Christian education. They have a Dutch school and English school in the city. At Zeeland, a Dutch school, and will soon have an English one and all the rest will follow. The teachers "must" be godly persons, who besides teaching reading and writing, must see that the children are prepared on the Catechism, and that they are taught to sing the Psalms. The ministers catechise all the children once a week, and if they are hindered, the elders take their place.

The pecuniary resources of the church are very low. The funds of the people, which were very limited, have been exhausted in the purchase of land, and in making their improvements, private and public, until there is nothing left. The pastors have had but little support, some of them literally none, from their churches. They have been obliged to struggle, and work, and suffer wants, just as these people have done. But they live in faith and hope of better times. They rejoice that the Lord has kept them alive and given them joy over their flocks in the dark and untrodden wilderness.

At the classical meeting it was soon made known that the brethren were a little afraid of entering into ecclesiastical connection with us although they believe in the union of brethren and sigh for Christian sympathy and association. They have so felt into the quick the galling chain of ecclesiastical domination and have seen with sorrow how exact organization according to human rules leads to formality on the one hand and to the oppression of tender consciences on the other that they hardly know what to say. I protested, of course, that it was the farthest from our thoughts to bring them in bondage to men or to exercise an ecclesiastical tyranny over them. And I stated that they would be most perfectly free at any time they found an ecclesiastical connection opposed to their religious prosperity or enjoyment to bid us a fraternal adieu and be by themselves again.

On comparison of doctrine a perfect agreement with our standards was found. In the order of their churches they believe each church and consistory shall direct and manage its own concerns; and incline to the idea that an appellate jurisdiction of superior judicatories is not so scriptural as kind and fraternal conferences and advice. Each of their churches appoint as many elders as seem desirable and they are always in office until they are dismissed as guilty and unworthy or removed by death. As the result they agreed with these explanations to join our Synod. It was deemed best that they should not emerge themselves into our existing Classis of Michigan, but unite as a separate Classis with our classes there. To this agreement I saw no insuperable objection and I would report the Classis of Holland accordingly.

On the subject of missionary aid the brethren expressed most singular and honorable objections. They thought it seemed best that the obligation of the churches to support them as pastors should not be impaired by the hope of foreign aid and that until the churches were able suitably to take care of their pastors, they must suffer with their people. That they were all sadly poor was true but they saw no example in the Scripture, in which a suffering church or people asked for aid, and therefore did not feel at liberty in their correspondence to dot it. But there was a precedent in the Scriptures in which, when it was known that the churches of Judea suffered, other churches sent them supplies not as by solicitation but out of brotherly love and bounty. If therefore our churches, knowing by this report how straitened they were, would out of their love and sympathy send a free gift to the Colony to be appropriated as the ministers and elders should deem the necessities of the saints demanded they would receive and acknowledge it with all gratitude in the Lord.

I felt that this was taking high and holy ground and I hope it may be considered within the powers of the missionary board to meet their hallowed scruples in this matter. And whether the board can do this or not there is one form in which they can minister to the necessity of the emigrants and in this form I adventured to take the liberty to pledge their aid. There are scattering companies of Hollanders at Kalamazoo, Grandville, Grand Haven, Allegan, and a number of surrounding places, which the brethren in the Colony endeavor to supply. But this supply is extremely inconvenient and laborious for them. For example, Allegan is thirty miles and Kalamazoo still further from the Colony. The ministers have no horses, and to walk afoot thirty miles out and preach three times on the Sabbath is very exhausting work when they must clamber their way often by blazed trees and along Indian trails. The bretheren very much wished they had a missionary or itinerant brother who should have these small and scattered flocks under his soled care. I promised that as soon as they could call a suitable man and report to you, you would put him on the footing of your most favored country missionaries. The Rev. Mr. Klyn will come through New York. He has sacrificed much to this service.

The Graafschap to which he is called is struggling with difficulties. Any token of love from you or the New York churches to him will be very opportune.

The length of time necessarily spent in Michigan had already thrown me a week beyond my engagement to return and it became out of my power to visit the settlements and churches in Wisconsin. I made a visit to Milwaukee and spent the Sabbath with the churches there. There are about sixty Holland families, comprising seventy-five communicants mostly located on the south side of Milwaukee River, where they have built a very decent house of worship. They have no minister at present, and they compelled me to attempt to preach to them in the Holland language. Then I ascertained that there is a church in the neighborhood of Sheboygan under the care of the Rev. Peter Zonne embracing about eighty families and perhaps the same number of communicants.

At Waupun, six miles from Fond-du-lac, the head of the Winebago Lake, there is a settlement of thirty families or more and a regularly organized church under the care of the Rev. Mr. [Gerrit] Baay, containing more than forty members.

There is also a rising settlement eight or ten miles out of Milwaukee, consisting of sixteen families who have neither organization nor minister. I am informed by letter from Mr. B. of the willingness of himself and church to connect themselves with our church and their thankfulness for any aid our missionary board may please to give. I have written to him, advising him to join the Holland Classis until a Wisconsin Classis can be formed.

On my return, I ascertained, that there was a sufficient number of Holland emigrants at Buffalo, to form a respectable church; - that they had been just ready to organize under the ministry of the Rev. Cornelius van Malsen, a most godly and estimable young man, when it pleased God to remove him by death, and that no other movement has since been made among them. There is also an organized church at Pickleville and Pultneyville, eighteen miles from Rochester, under care of the presbytery of Streutren, to which the Rev. John Visscher has been sent as a missionary by the Home Missionary Society of the Old School Presbyterian Church.

There is another organized church of Hollanders at Rochester under care of presbytery, to which the Rev. A. B. Veenhuysen ministers. Your commissioner felt a disagreeable emotion at the thought, that these Holland brethren, agreeing with our church in every particular of standards, doctrine, and government, should have been so long neglected by us, that at last they must fall into the hands of strangers to their language and customs. But still, thanks are due to God, and to our Presbyterian brethren, that the poor people were provided with the bread of life.

On the whole I consider the Holland colony in Michigan most wisely located in divine providence. There are many excellent men in the state who cordially favor its interests. The state has enacted a law appropriating 3,000 acres of land to make roads in the colony and 4,000 for the erection of a pier and other facilities for convenience. The ministers and the city council importuned me till I could not refuse to promise them as soon as possible to negotiate for them the loan of a thousand dollars on the whole property of the city, consisting of eleven contiguous eighty acre lots for the purpose of building this pier. A spirit of brotherly kindness and philanthropy reigns among these colonists which must be as acceptable before God as it is beautiful before me. A case will illustrate this. Two godly parents having six children both died leaving no relations or support for their orphans. Immediately six families adopted each one of the orphans, to bring them up in all respects as their own and one of their families (brother Van Raalte has six of his own). It is a most remarkable community and God will sustain and bless it and I feel that it will be a blessing and an honor to us to be His instruments in this matter.

In conclusion if I have been more particular and prolix in the report than is usual, I think you will pardon me. I judge you wish not for generalities but for particulars and I have endeavored to furnish them. My journey has been very fatiguing but if you should have as much pleasure in hearing and ministering as I have had in observing and detailing we shall all be amply repaid for this effort of Christian benevolence.

Respectfully Submitted,

Isaac N. Wyckoff

Deputy of the Missonary Society

THE REMINISCENCES OF AREND JAN BRUSSE

(This account of emigration from Arnhem to Milwaukee, Wisc. in 1846 was first published in 1946 in the Wisconsin Magazine of History, XXIX, being based on a manuscript preserved in the Netherlands Museum)

When I was a young man, aged about twenty-two years, from what I noticed of the general condition of the class of people to whom I belonged I plainly saw that my temporal prospects for life were not very promising in the Netherlands; and so I concluded to go to America, if I possibly could get there. I then had no idea that my parents and the rest of my family would break up and also go to America; but my mother, not being willing to let me go alone, induced father that we all go together. Our family consisted of father and mother: Jan Brusse, and his wife Grada, with their seven children, Arend Jan, Gerrit Jan, Dersse, Willem, Berend, Janna, and Hendrik.

On the first day of June 1846 we left our home at Dinxperloo, province of Gelderland, for Rotterdam; by way of Arnhem and the Rhine. At Rotterdam we took passage on the sailing vessel De Hollander. There were 100 passengers on board, of whom one-half were Hollanders; the others were Germans. Of the ten families of Hollanders seven came from Aalten, Varseveld, and Dinxperloo, from what is known as de Achterhoek. The others came from Velp near Arnhem and from the province of Zeeland.

Of the many Hollanders on board the ship I had only been intimately acquainted with Rademaker and family, from Varseveld. He was one of the elders of the Reformed (Afgescheiden) Church of Varseveld, a gifted and devout Christian. Of this church I had been a catechumen till I left for America, and of which I still retain many blessed memories. On board the ship everything was about as inconvenient and as untidy or dirty as it could be. We were herded together almost like cattle. We had to provide our own provisions for the voyage. There was little chance for cooking. The stove, or range, or whatever you might call it, had only two or three holes, where the many families could do their cooking. The water for drinking and cooking was nasty. I yet imagine that I can smell it. Those who did attempt cooking on the stove were not always particular about the fire. At one time through someone's carelessness the ship took fire, and but for its timely discovery might have turned out very serious. We had only one severe storm that was considered really dangerous. and when we left the ship there was one more passenger than when we boarded it.

After being forty days on the Atlantic Ocean we landed at Boston. Our aim, and that of the seven families mentioned above, was to reach Milwaukee, Wisconsin. But how to get there was a serious question. There we were, strangers in a strange land; we understood nobody, and nobody understood us. I could speak a little German, and so could Roelof Sleijster, one of our fellow passengers. Well, as best we could we made a bargain with a German agent to get us to Milwaukee. Through

81

our ignorance we knew nothing of the route we were to travel. This was in 1846, hence we were among the very first that left old Holland to open the way to the West.

At   Boston we were put into the cars of a freight train that slowly took us to Albany. Arriving at Albany we had to stay there for a day, and stopped at a German hotel. While there the Rev. Dr. Isaac N. Wyckoff passed by. Hearing us speaking Dutch, he stopped and took some of us to his home. There Sleijster who had been a theological student at Arnhem gave Dr. Wyckoff a letter from the Rev. A. C. van Raalte and the Rev. A. Brummelkamp   [dated Arnhem, June 1846]   directed <u>Aan de Geloovigen in de Vereenigde Staten van Noord-Amerika</u> (To the Faithful in the United States of North America). Through this medium the Hollanders became acquainted with the Reformed Church in America.

At Albany we got on an immigrant canal boat. The horses going nearly always on a walk; in the day time, I walked a good deal of the time by the side of the boat. It was a slow and tedious way of traveling. Our daily fare on the boat was bread and milk, which we bought along the route of the canal. After being a week on the canal boat we reached Buffalo. From there, as steerage passengers on a steamer, we came to Milwaukee late in July 1846.

The only Hollander we met in Milwaukee was a saloonkeeper by the name of Wessink. He told us that times in Milwaukee were dull and advised us to go into the country among the farmers. There was a farmer at his place from near Kenosha who had come to Milwaukee for help on his big farm, or farms, it being wheat harvest time. Through this Holland saloonkeeper we made a bargain with the farmer. He promised to give us work through the harvest, and after that was finished we were to continue working for him, or take his farm and work it. We hired a team and followed the farmer to within sight of Kenosha, where at the semblage of a house, we unloaded our goods and took possession.

This farmer had a large field of wheat. He was to give every one of the family work, or to those of us that could work. He tried us, to see what we could do. My brother Gerrit did not like the appearance of things; so, he went to work for another farmer. The rest of us were set to work. I and two other hands were sent into the fields with cradles to cut grain; it was the hardest work I ever did. I found that this farmer was a dishonest rascal. When his grain was cut, we had to leave, without getting a cent for our hard and honest work. We again hired teams and went back to Milwaukee. By this time our purse was getting light and I had to do something. I got work tending a bricklayer, made mortar, carried brick, etc; and again I was cheated out of my pay.

In Milwaukee I had become acquainted with a Zeelander, a painter, by the name of Lukwilder, who had been in this country for years. He persuaded me to go into the painting business with his boss, and I did so. After having worked at this for a number of weeks, painting made me sick and I had to quit. Again I got no pay for this work. I felt that I was yet far from the promised land. In fact I was almost ready to exclaim, as I later heard Dominie Hendrik Geert Klijn exclaim (the gentle dominie) when a boat of Hollanders destined for Holland, Michigan, stopped at Milwaukee longer than he thought necessary, and he seemed to think there was a sinister motive in this delay, "O dit goddelooze Amerika" (Oh this wicked America!)

Milwaukee was then a town of 6,000 people. On the Northwest part of the town away from the Milwaukee River bottoms which then were covered with stumps, and in the spring stood under water, but now form the center of that beautiful city there was a commons where most of the Hollanders who had come with us across the sea were living in cabins. So we settled there. I helped build our cabin 16 feet square, out of rough common lumber. The boards were lapped and nailed on like siding, without anything else being added inside or out, and the roof was of the same material. There was also a so-called upstairs which was reached by climbing a homemade ladder. Not much of a manse this - and it was certainly an uncomfortable dwelling during a storm or in weather below zero.

We few Hollanders there keenly felt being deprived of the public ministry of the gospel of Jesus Christ to which we had been accustomed in Holland. As a substitute I suggested to our Holland friends that we meet on Sunday afternoons for worship in our cabin. To this they all agreed. This was the beginning of social life and public religious meetings among the Hollanders of Milwaukee.

Aside from prayer and song and the reading of Scripture, I made use of a volume of Hennenbroek's sermons from which some sermon was read. This certainly was a day of small things as far as means and outward form are concerned, but God's presence surely was felt.

Later in the fall of this same year, 1846, other families of Hollanders from the Old Country came to Milwaukee, so that by winter we had quite a settlement of Hollanders op den Hollandschen berg ("on Dutch hill") as the Hollanders used to call it. I do not know who was the owner of that land, but we were not disturbed.

A great bereavement befell us - my mother, who for years had been in poor health, died in October, three months after our landing. Care of the family devolved upon my sister Dersse, now Mrs. William Giebink of Waupun, Wisconsin, the only one of us children except the writer now living. On October 9, 1850, my father died from the effects of cholera which at that time was prevalent in many parts of the country. So after a short stay, after great privations and many hardships incident to a new country, both parents passed away.

That first winter in Milwaukee I had no steady employment, but my brother Gerrit who was a tailor readily got all the work he could do. In the summer of 1847, the Rev. Pieter Zonne with a number of families came from The Netherlands to Milwaukee. We rented a hall, and for over a year he preached to the Hollanders without pay. Zonne was certainly a talented preacher, whose ministry I greatly enjoyed. The population of Hollanders op den Hollandschen berg kept increasing all the time I lived in Milwaukee, but all of them were comparatively poor. In Scripture parlance, they were the hewers of wood and drawers of water for the well-to-do Yankees.

In Milwaukee I kept working at whatever I could find. Soon I began to go to an evening school, and for two years I attended a collegiate institute. It was my desire to enter the ministry of the gospel. I was given the opportunity to study at the Rochester University and Theological Seminary. There I was ordained to the ministry of the gospel of Jesus Christ. God indeed has ever been good to me.

Before I left Milwaukee in 1850 the Hollanders had learned that Uncle Sam had cheap and fertile lands which invited occupation. Some accordingly left for the timber lands of Seboygan County, where they each claimed a quarter section of land. These Hollanders at once started to turn the wilderness into fruitful fields and in time came to own their splendid farms.

When I left Milwaukee de Hollandsche berg began to assume a different appearance. Streets were laid out, lots were sold cheap, the humble cabins of the first pioneers were replaced by more pretentious and desirable dwellings, and we Hollanders realized that we really had come to a better country. We have great reason to be thankful to our heavenly Father for having led us to this land of plenty.

Now at the age of eighty - five years as I look back with my mind's eye to the first Hollanders as they came to this country, most of them poor, uneducated, and lacking in practically all of the civilities of American social life, I see them and their children, educated, enterprising, thrifty, and prosperous, equal in every way in social as well as in business life to any class of people in this broad land. May God continue to bless the Hollanders and their descendants in America, who remain true to the faith of our fathers.

P.S. I ought to state by way of explanation, that as my life and labors were among English-speaking people who pronounced my name "Bruce" instead of "Brusse", the newer spelling and pronunciation were adopted. Letters addressed to "Brusse" were invariably returned to the sender and for that reason I chose the form "Bruce".

CORNELIUS VAN LOO'S
ZEELAND TOWNSHIP AND VILLAGE

The territory included within the bounds of the township of Zeeland was in 1845 part of the township of Polkton. That was in the good old days when three men constituted the board of supervisors of Ottawa County. Timothy Eastman was supervisor. The total assessment was $12.359 and the total tax $41.78 on fourteen descriptions of land. One of these descriptions was the south-west quarter of section 28. On the east half of this quarter Jan Hulst settled, arriving there for permanent residence on June 8, 1847, being the first settler in the township. His son, Jan Hulst Jr., still lives on the same farm. One week later Hilbert Mast arrived and settled on the east section. The above named Jan Hulst left his home in the Netherlands March 2, 1847, left the port of Hellevoet March 19, and arrived at Baltimore, Maryland, April 27. From there the journey was over land to his farm, occupying six weeks.

The first settlers at or near the village were: Jan Steketee in July 1847, Jacobus de Hond, and Christiak den Herder of whom the latter arrived on August 16, 1847, and settled on the south-west quarter section 17. He brought with him a load of lumber and immediately placed it on end in the shape of a bell tent under which the family passed the first night in the wilderness. At that time the township was part of Georgetown Township, Asa A. Scott being supervisor; in 1848 it was part of Ottawa Township, C. B. Albee, supervisor; in 1849 part of Allendale Township, Grosvenor Reed, supervisor; in 1849-50 part of Holland Township, Henry D. Post, supervisor.

At a session of the legislature in 1850 Zeeland was organized as a separate township, and the first meeting was held July 14, 1851, and the following persons were elected township officers: supervisor, Elias G. Young; clerk and treasurer, Robbertus M. de Bruyn; directors of the poor, Hessel O. Yntema, Jan de Pree; highway commissioners, Milan Coburn, Robbertus M. de Bruyn, Sietse op't Holt; justices of the peace, J. Nieuwendorp, Elias G. Young, Johannes G. van Hees; constables, Hendrik de Kruif, George H. Baart, Willem Kremers. Number of votes cast, 93.

First general election held under the new constitution of 1850 was also held in 1851, when sixty-five votes were cast, 57 Democratic and 8 Whig. In 1852 the presidential election was held, and 141 votes cast, 131 were Democratic and ten Whig.

In October 1853 Arie van Bree was appointed agent for the sale of spirituous liquors under the new liquor law at an annual salary of $15. A stock of $20 worth of liquors was procured which he was scarcely able to sell under the stringent provisions of the law. The total number of accounts allowed against the town the first year was $111.99.

December 26, 1850, the first school district was organized, and the first school meeting was held in the Reformed church building January 7, 1851. Johannes G. van Hees was elected moderator, Robbertus M. de Bruyn, director, and Hendrik de Kruif, assessor. One dollar tax was voted for each child between four and eighteen years of age.

At the first meeting of the board of school inspectors Elias G. Young was examined and licensed as teacher, and a week later Madame Young also. August 15, 1851, Rev. Cornelius van der Meulen visited the Zeeland school, and Robbertus M. de Bruyn visited the Vriesland school in district number two, then recently organized. This was the first official school and Robbertus M. de Bruyn visited the Vriesland school in district number two, then recently organized. This was the first official school visitation had in the township.

The first highway in the town was laid out November 23, 1849, excepting the state road from Grandville to Holland, angling through the town and long since taken up. C. B. Albee and Frank B. Gilbert were the commissioners that laid out the first highway with Timothy Eastman, surveyor. In March 1851 Henry D. Post and James Walker, commissioners, and Bernardus Grootenhuis, surveyor, laid out and recorded fourteen highways in the town providing an outlet to most of the settlers.

The first child born was one of Cornelius Weninger, though the first of which there is an official record was Wouter van Nuil, September 18, 1847, and, according to the church record, baptized in October.

The first couple married were Jan Wabeke and Martina Glerum, December 1, 1847, by Rev. Cornelius van der Meulen, at the house of the latter. The witnesses were Jannes van de Luyster and Jan Stekeete. All the parties to this interesting ceremony are now deceased.

In Vriesland the first couple to enter into the bonds of matrimony were John van Zoeren and lady, both still living.

Jan Elsma on section twenty-two was the first settler in that part of the town in July 1847. He is still living and knows what house building means. First he made himself comfortable under a brush tent, then in a log house, next a frame, and now he inhabits a substantial brick building. He is a typical old country Frisian, quaint, individual, religious, patriotic, and republican, as all Frisians are, loyal to all that is noble, beautiful, and true.

The first settlers of Zeeland all came from the land of William the Silent, bringing with them the love of liberty, civil and religious, of the great prince. The secession of a large body of Christians from the dead formalism of the state church in the Netherlands led to persecution by fine, imprisonment, loss of employment, and obliquy. Free church and free schools, freedom to worship God according to the dictates of their own conscience, and a desire to improve their temporal conditions, finally led them to forsake the land of their birth and to try their fortunes in a new world.

Early in 1847 three meetings were held in the little city of Goes in the province of Zeeland to consider the matter. It was decided to emigrate in a body. They organized themselves into a church society and elected Jannes van de Luyster and Johannes Hoogesteger as elders. It was further decided that they ought not to go without a minister, and extended a call to Cornelius van der Meulen of Goes, who accepted the call.

Three vessels left the Netherlands with the emigrants on board; the first under leadership of Jan Steketee, the second of Rev. Cornelius van der Meulen, and the third of Jannes van de Luyster, arriving here at different times during the summer of 1847. So it may be said that the Reformed church of Zeeland was organized in the old country, and came here as a church, the only known instance of the kind, with the exception of, perhaps, the pilgrim fathers.

In the eastern part of the township the first settlers were mainly from the province of Friesland, and also brought a minister with them, the Rev. Maarten Anne Ypma. The large family of Van Zoeren, however, came from Gelderland, and from this fact their neighborhood is still called De Geldersche Buurt. It will be noticed that the early settlers perpetuated the names of the different provinces when they came here, by applying them to the localities where they settled. Thus we have Holland, North Holland, Vriesland, Overisel, Graafschap, Old and New Groningen, Drenthe, Zeeland, and names of towns as Niekerk, Zutphen, Borculo, Hjderwijk, etc.

Jannes van de Luyster the proprietor of the village of Zeeland, bought of the United States government the entire section nineteen, on which the village is mainly located. He also bought section seventeen, which was settled mainly by his children, and peasantry of his farm in the old country, whom he brought with him.

Jan Wabeke, father of the late Rev. Cornelius Wabeke, also brought a number of poor families with him.

Jan Smallegange did the same in 1849 whereof the writer then ten years old was a humble member and who will hold the name of Smallegange in grateful remembrance while memory lasts.

Of the sufferings, privations, and struggles of these early settlers no one not familiar with pioneer life can form any conception. Locating in a dense wilderness without means, without roads, unacquainted with the language or institutions of the country, inexperienced in the severe toil required to clear up heavy timber land, suffering from diseases incident to the living around the swamps and to the process of acclimation. Many gave up the struggle and moved to Grand Rapids, Kalamazoo, Grand Haven, and other places some to return again when better days dawned. The majority, however, were "stayers", chief of whom was the old minister, Van der Meulen.

Poor as any other of the settlers with a family to support, he was at once minister, doctor, land-looker, and judge. When worn and tired and discouraged, the colonists came out of the woods from different directions on Sabbath mornings, the old saint of God would preach to them with a pathos and a fervid eloquence now seldom heard, and would send them back in the evening to their humble cabins with new courage, with firmer purpose and more unfaltering trust, to renew the struggle in the forest and hew out a home and competence. Before any one had a decent house to live in these sturdy men of Puritan mould built a church of hewn timbers, 40 by 60 feet, the most substantial and most comfortable building in all the settlement. Nor was the school forgotten, for though school district No. I was not organized, in a legal way, till December 26, 1850, yet a school was taught long before that, part of the time by a man who came there to sell fruit trees, and afterwards by Robbertus M. de Bruyn, father of Rev. Pieter de Bruyn, who was probably the first Hollander qualified to teach school in Ottawa County. And let us note here while speaking of schools that it has ever been the endeavor of the settlers in this township to have a free school of American type. They have never been led off into sectarian or parochial bypaths, not even to the idea of a school taught in the Holland language for which it seems our fellow citizens of the same nationality in other localities have a penchant. While not ashamed of the land of their fathers but proud of their ancestry and loving the language in which their forefathers worshipped God, wooed their brides, and recited the deeds of Tromp and De Ruyter, Mauritz and William the Silent to their wondering children, yet they do not believe in a Holland or a France, an Ireland, or a Germany in free America. Again, while clinging to their church and their doctrines with tenacity and respecting their ministers and giving them generous support, yet must it be said in justice to Zeeland's inhabitants, that they are as free from sectarian spirit and bigotry as any equal body of citizens in the United States. They are most intensely jealous of their right to think for themselves on every subject; loyal to the core to the land of their adoption, and thorough believers in its free institutions. In proportion to their means they are generous to prodigality toward suffering humanity and lead all other Holland communities in support of domestic and foreign missions.

Quite a number of young men of our township served in the civil war; among those killed were Dirk Keppel, Gerrit van Bree, and Alexander Jonkheer. The township paid out $25,180,30 for the support of the war for the Union. The township also paid large sums toward the opening of Holland harbor.

The disastrous fire of 1871, when Holland was laid in ashes, taxed the generosity to the utmost, while at a township meeting held in 1880 a sum of $800 was raised for the relief of the sufferers by the fires in the state during August and September of that year.

The Russian famine of the present winter again touched the sympathies of the people, and almost without effort, over 300,000 pounds of flour was collected and sent forward on its errand of relief and mercy.

Zeeland village is situated on the west line of the township, and was platted in 1849. At present it contains 780 inhabitants. School district number one, which includes the village, has a school census of 465 The village has three churches, the Reformed, and the First and Second Holland Christian Reformed, a fine two story school building with six school rooms, two furniture stores, two clothing stores, five general and one grocery store, one book store, two butcher shops, two wagon and smith shops, one hotel, one tannery, one cooper's shop, two flour exchange and feed stores and a fine furniture factory, which turns out over $1,000 worth of suites and side boards every week. The village is on sections 18 and 19, township 5 north, range 14 west, on the Chicago and West Michigan Railway, and is twenty miles southwest of Grand Rapids, twenty-six from the country seat. On section three is situated Beaverdam church and postoffice and two stores; on section 15 the Reformed church building of Vriesland, one of the largest and finest church buildings to be found outside of a village or city. A fine brick school building stands just across from the church, and on the opposite corner is the fine store of Den Herder and Tanis, and the Vriesland cheese factory near by. On the corner of section 34 is the Drenthe Christian Reformed Church, a brick school house and the large store of H.

Bakker and Son. On the opposite corner is a general store in which is kept the Drenthe postoffice, with a blacksmith shop and wagon shop in the immediate vicinity.

The population of the township outside of the village of Zeeland is 2,236, making a total in the town of about 3,000. In 1854 it was 912. In 1874 it was 2,576. Since the first presidential vote, which stood Democratic 131, Whig 10, there has been a great change in the politics of the town, receiving its first impetus in the trying period of the war, and constantly fostered by discussion and effective work. It may safely be stated that there is more politics to the square foot in Zeeland, year in and year out, than in any other locality in the state. In 1876 the vote stood: Republican 296, Democratic 147; 1880, Republican 348, Democratic 132; 1884, Republican 371, Democratic 162; 1888, Republican 430, Democratic 184. The reasons for this condition and political complexion of the town are: first, the Democratic party's record on secession and rebellion, finance and tariff; second, the intense jealousy with which the Zeelanders regard their civil and religious rights and our public school system, all of which they regard in constant danger from the Catholic hierarchy which, together with the liquor interest of the country, is a standing menace to free institutions.

ADRIAN JOHNSON'S
HOLLANDERS IN GRAND RAPIDS

To write a historical paper on any subject one should have some documentary resources to draw from, but as I have none, I have to write mostly from my own memory, and from what I could gather from other old people.

When I arrived in Grand Rapids on the 5th day of August 1849 I found a few Hollanders here, namely, Frans van Driele, Louis Lageweg, Barteld Luten, John Roost, Josiah (Josua) Elenbaas, John Hendricks and family, Paulus d'Ooge, Adriaan Semeyn, and a few others, and some young girls who were working as domestics.

I could not learn the name of the Hollander who first arrived in Grand Rapids, but her history was told me by Thomas B. Church, who is dead now, but who was well known among the Hollanders.

In 1847 a young girl came here by stage from Kalamazoo (the only means of transportation we had at that time) and was left at the National Hotel. She could not speak a word of English, and she went to work for a family by the name of Peasley. The girl was melancholy and seemed to be in distress about something. Mrs. Peasley tried to find out her trouble but as she could not talk with the girl, she called in some foreigners who were in Grand Rapids at that time. None of them could speak her language, and Mrs. Peasley finally called Mr. Church, who had some knowledge of a few foreign languages, but he could not understand the girl. He told Mrs. Peasley he would write to Ds. van Raalte and tell him about the girl. When Ds. van Raalte came to Grand Rapids Mr. Church took him to Mrs. Peasley's to the girl, and as soon as she heard her native tongue she forgot all who surrounded her and embraced and kissed the little man in the presence of all. Then they started a conversation, in which she stated that her lover had written her that he was in Grand Rapids, and had sent her money to enable her to remove to this country and that he had directed her to come to Grand Rapids. She did not find her lover, nor anybody else whom she could talk to. Mr. Church suggested to Ds. van Raalte as there was also a Grand Rapids in Wisconsin , that he correspond with somebody in Grand Rapids, Wisconsin, and find out whether there was such a young man in that city. Shortly after this the young man came, took his bride, and they went their way rejoicing.

I have cited this episode to show the difficulties which the first emigrants had to contend with, and the services of the eminent Van Raalte were needed everywhere.

The first Holland settlers of Grand Rapids were but a small body among the Americans, and some of the sharp Yankees would often take advantage of the Hollanders' ignorance of the English language.

I recollect that my father worked for a man who kept a general store, where he had to take all his earnings out in trade. One day my mother wanted some meat, not seeing it in the store, (she had to point at everything she wanted), she asked a Holland neighbor how to say "spek en vleesch" in English. Her friend told her to call for "pork and beef," and my father and mother went to the store, repeating on the way the names of the much desired articles. When they came at the store and asked for it, the storekeeper pretended he did not understand them, and he showed them white beans and clover seed!

I met a friend of mine the other day. We were talking about olden times, and he told me how he one day met an American who asked him, "Dutchman, you want work?" Thinking the man asked him if he had work, he answered "no". A few days later another man asked if he wanted work, and by way of inducement told him that he would pay "cash", which was a great inducement, as most of us were paid in store orders, but my friend told him that he did not want to work for "kaas", being under the impression that he would be obliged to take his pay in cheese, the man hailing from the province of Zeeland, where they pronounce the word "kaas" somewhat like the English word "cash".

But it must be said to the honor of the Americans that they used a great deal of patience with us and they preferred the Hollanders to the English-speaking laborers who were here, because the Hollanders were industrious and honest.

Money was scarce in those days. We all had to take our pay in store orders. I myself worked nine months for one man, my wages being $ 8 per month and board, and all the money I received during that time was $ 6.

The first marriage ceremonies, as near as I can ascertain, were performed by Rev. Martin Ypma from Vriesland, the contracting parties being Klaas Kloosterhuis and Lamigjen Vredeveld, and Roelof Kloosterhuis and Diena Mulder. They were married at the house of Frans van Driele.

I do not know much about the first births and deaths, for the records of Kent county were destroyed by the fire in 1857, but I was told that the first death that occurred was of a man of the name of Bos. He died in Parish Township, and as the people knew of no burying ground, they buried him right there on the farm. He was afterwards taken up by friends and interred in a burying ground. Many Hollanders were buried in the potter's field of the Fulton Street cemetery, and their resting places will never be found or known until the day of resurrection.

The first sad calamity happening to a Holland family here was an accident which befell a promising young man by the name of Cornelius Stoutjesdyk. He came to Grand Rapids with his parents in 1849, being 11 years old. After being here a while, he hired out as an apprentice to learn the mason trade with Mr. Louis Davidson. On the 22nd day of June 1857 he fell from a four-story window of the Lovett block, which was then in course of erection, to the sidewalk below, and was picked up dead. This event spread sadness among the Holland settlers, for, as I have said before, he was a very promising young man, and had a bright future before him. He was but 19 years old and engaged to be married to Mary Adriaanse. Almost the whole population, Hollanders and Americans, attended the funeral, the services being conducted by the venerable Rev. H. G. Klyn, and I never attended a funeral before or since where there were so many tears shed as at this one, it being the first calamity of that kind which ever happened in Grand Rapids, and it is still remembered by many old settlers.

One of the early noted Holland settlers was Peter J. G. Hodenpyl, who came to this country in 1840, and was professor in languages in Rutgers College, in New Brunswick, New Jersey, from 1842 to 1846. He came to

Ravenna, then in Ottawa, now in Muskegon County, in 1846. A man by the name of Edmond B. Bostwick had bought a number of sections of land there with the intention of starting a Holland colony. Hodenpyl, formerly having been connected with a foreign emigration bureau in New York, and being acquainted with Mr. Bostwick, was prevailed upon to come to Ravenna to start the colony.

Some Hollanders of Grand Rapids went out there; and Rev. Huibertus Jacobus Budding came to this country with some Holland emigrants, who after arriving in New York sent them also to Ravenna. The first Hollanders who went there from Grand Rapids were Johannes Hendricks, Paulus and Adrian d'Ooge, Cornelius Borrendamme, and a few others; but they never bought any land. The Hollanders who came with Rev. Budding to Ravenna were Adriaan Pleune, Cornelius van Sliederegt, Jacob Gouw, Jacob de Waal, and some others whose names I have forgotten. They took up a piece of land, but had nothing to begin with, not even a thing to eat, and at first endured many hardships. They lived on turnips boiled in water without salt or seasoning whatever, for fifteen days. They all lived in the same log shanty, which had been used for stabling oxen, and they built a fire in the center of the shanty, and having no soap to wash with, the smoke soon made them look like darkies, so in the midst of their misery they had to laugh at one another's appearance. I myself went there in January 1851 and found these people settled on their land. I had nothing to eat but dry johnnycake for a month. But as these people had taken up their land on contract and were not able to pay interest, they all left the settlement and the improvements which they had made upon it, and came to Grand Rapids. I bought Van Sliederegt's contract for a calf, an old silver watch, two geese, and a jackknife; but as they all moved to Grand Rapids, I went with them and have never seen the land since. Thus the Holland colony in Ravenna was a failure. I have inserted this bit of history in this paper, because it has some connection with the early settlers of Grand Rapids.

Since 1848 the Holland population of Grand Rapids has increased from a very few to about 25,000. And from the gathering of a few people   we had not yet organized a congregation   , in the stone church on East Bridge Street, where Frans van Driele lived in one end of the basement and services were held in the other, we have now twenty-five organized congregations. The Hollanders had the honor of building the first brick church in Grand Rapids.

The old Holland settlers, with the exception of a few, have all saved money enough to live comfortably in their old age.

As I am not a historian, nor a student of history, nor even a scholar, because my parents were poor and my education was very limited, this paper is, of course, very incomplete. But I hope the committee will be satisfied.

In the issue of De Grondwet, of July 4, 1911, appeared an article on "The Early Settlement of Ravenna, Michigan," by Professor Martin Luther D'ooge (No. 41 of these Memoirs). It is this same effort at colonization that reference is made to in the foregoing article. The Grand River Eagle, in its issue of February 1, 1849, also makes mention of the enterprise set on foot by Mr. Hodenpyl, as follows:

"We have taken some pains to find out the present situation and future prospects of the Holland colony, established at Ravenna, on Crockery Creek, in the northern portion of Ottawa County.

"There are about eighty souls, all told, but they are pioneers of large numbers who will follow them the coming spring. Many of the present settlers have purchased land, and are preparing for spring crops.

"Mr. Hodenpyl, who leads the colony, is an enterprising man and an educated gentleman. He is erecting a grist mill at Ravenna for the purpose of giving aid to the infant colony.

"There are three agents in Holland for the purpose of bringing out emigrants early next season, to make their future home among us, and, from the high toned recommendations of the country by those already located, no doubt thousands will follow.

"A large number of small frame buildings are to be put up on the road leading from Steel's Landing to Ravenna, ready for settlers the coming spring. Each of these buildings to be placed a quarter of a mile from the other, and five acres of land to be cleared off and fenced about each house. This land is to be cleared off forty rods along the road, and twenty rods back, so that half of the forest will at once disappear along the public highway for a distance of three miles, commencing one mile south of the mills at Ravenna and extending three miles toward Steel's Landing."
---Gerrit van Schelven.

In giving you, on the occasion of this Semi-Centennial Celebration of the Holland Immigration in the United States, a historical sketch of Sayville, the chief interest of course centres in the settlement of the Hollanders there. For a clear understanding of our subject I deem it necessary to tooch briefly upon the place and its environment.

Sayville is situated, as you are aware, on Long Island which is a part of New York State. The first settlement on the island was made in 1625, under Dutch protection, by some French Protestants, who founded an asylum here to worship God according to the dictates of their conscience. The first settler was George Jansen de Rapalje, and his daughter Sarah was the first white child to be born on Long Island. In 1636 several Hollanders settled at its western end near New York while the larger part, especially its eastern section, was populated by New Englanders and for the most by people from Connecticut. Its length from the East River to Montauk Point is 125 miles, and its average breadth 14 miles, with an area of 162 square miles. By reason of its length the Hollanders called it "Lange Eiland", which the English in 1693 changed by law to "Island of Nassau". This name, however, never came into popular use, so that it is still known by its original appelation. It is noted for its picturesque coast indented by numerous bays and inlets as also for its splendid villages and watering places, together with several lighthouses, and it has some 30 lifesaving stations.

Sayville is situated 50 miles East from New York City, in the town of Islip, Suffolk County. Islip derives its name from a small town in England. It was settled back in 1666 when a patent was granted to the inhabitants of Satuaket by Governor Nicholie, which grant was reaffirmed by Governor Donnegan in 1686, reserving to the crown all lands not purchased by them from the Indians. Sayville is near the Great South Bay, with a frontage of one and a half miles, and about five miles from the Atlantic Ocian. Between the bay and the ocean stretches a narrow strip of land, 30 miles long. Fire Island - so named, it is said, because formerly nightly fires at times were kindled by pirates on its beach for the purpose of wrecking ships in order to plunder them.

Seaville, or village by the sea, was the original name intended for this beautiful village. The citizens, at a meeting in 1836, concluded it was time to ask Uncle Sam to give the hamlet a name and a post office; but by some mistake the clerk at Washington who copied the petition wrote "Sayville", and so it has remained to this day. Its first settlers were Willet Green and John Edwards. The names of Green and Edwards are still common in and around Sayville. In 1847, two years settlers were Willet Green and John Edwards. The names of Green and Edwards are still common in and around Sayville. In 1847, two years before any Hollander arrived here, the first church, the Methodist Episcopal, was built; in 1849 the Congregational; in 1866 the Episcopal; and in 1896 the Catholic. The original Methodist and Congregational structures have since been succeeded by attractive, handsome, and substantial edifices. While on the subject of churches, I can state that before any church was erected in Sayville, there existed and still exists–though no longer in use– a church, two miles West from Sayville, at what is now Oakdale. It is the St. John's Episcopal Church built several years before the war of the Revolution. A few weeks ago a prominent wedding was solemnized in that church. The population of Sayville and its surrounding regions, though mainly composed of Americans, also had a goodly sprinkling of Hollanders, Germans, Irish, and Bohemians.

Our chief industry, like that of other Long Island towns, is shell fishing - oysters in winter and clams in summer. The land around Sayville is, on the whole, poor, sandy soil, not suitable for farming unless heavily manured. It is, besides, too dear for agricultural purposes, as most of it is in the hands of the rich, like the van der Bilts, Cuttings, and others belonging to the South Side Club, who are loath to part with it. These lands are covered with either primeval or second growth forests, abounding in smaller kinds of game. But deer also roam through these woods to the no small detriment of the farmers on the outskirts. Large droves are frequently seen in the evening on the public road two miles west from Sayville. According to the game laws of the State of New York deer are allowed to be hunted each Wednesday during every week in November.

Speaking of the shellfish industry. I mention the fact that in the first part of the present century our oysters - known then and now as "Blue Points" - were famous for their size and flavor; and on account of their scarcity sold in New York for $ 5 a hundred, while a common laborer could get but 60 or 75 cents a day and a good mechanic only $1. In 1848 the oyster industry began to flourish and has since been developed more extensively. The Long Island Railroad was extended through Sayville in 1867. In educational matters we are in no ways behind other towns of its size. We have as fine a High School as is met with in any country place, employing ten or eleven first class teachers who are all able to prepare their pupils for college.

The first Hollanders in Sayville were Cornelius De Waal and Cornelius Hage who came here in 1849. Hage turned his attention to farming, but De Waal bought a boat in which he conveyed oysters and clams to market in New York. De Waal's brother Jacob who arrived with him in America at the same time went on with his family to Ravenna, Michigan, settling on a farm, having D'Ooge and Hodenpyl as neighbors; but in 1852 removed to Sayville. His son Gabriel is still living here with his family. Mrs. Jacob de Waal resided a number of years in Grand Rapids, Michigan, being married to Jacob de Haas, her second husband.

Prior to these arrivals a couple of Holland families - Verney and Hiddink - were living at Lake Land, a few miles outside Sayville. Verney brought his wagon and plow and other farming implements with him from across the ocean, thinking these tools were not to be had in America. After the beginnings of a settlement had been made, Hollanders immigrated hither, the greater part of them from the province of Zeeland, where having made their living by shell, they speedily recognized their opportunities in Sayville.

Although not kindly received by the native population who did not favor foreigners and viewed them as intruders, the Hollanders struggled on quietly and patiently, persevering in what they had undertaken. Having put their hand to the plow they never looked back. They did not try to get to the top of the ladder at once, but began to climb from the lowest rung. They bought old boats from the Americans, worth from $100 to $150, and with those went about their business. Gradually they succeeded, for at present they are the owners not only of splendid boats, valued at from $700 to $1,000, but also control the shell-fishing business in and around Sayville. The first extensive oyster shipper among them was Dirk van Wyen, now deceased.

Every spring, at an enormous outlay of money, the Hollanders plant thousands of bushels of oysters in the Bay, and take them up during the autumn and winter months. The Blue Point oysters, besides being much sought after wherever known, are shipped not only to all points of our own country, but also to Europe, the greater part being taken by England. Our wide awake oyster planters and shippers are Jacob Ockers, the Westerheke Brothers, the Van der Borgh Brothers, John van Wyen, Wolfert van Popering, and William Rudolph.

Lest I should leave a mistaken impression, I wish to remark here that for the majority of the Hollanders live in West Sayville instead of Sayville. We have a post office of our own and two churches-one Reformed and one Christian Reformed. The two places are separated by a narrow stretch of marshy woodland through which flows a limpid crystal brook whose outlet is in the Bay. The population of the two villages is between 2000 and 2500. According to the census of 1875 there were 328 Hollanders including their children. We may estimate that at present there are between 500 and 600 of them.

Having thus far treated the material interests of Sayville, especially as regards the Hollanders, my sketch would be incomplete if I failed to notice its religious aspects. From the beginning of their settling here, the Hollanders held religious services on the Lord's day. They would meet in someone's house and one of their number would read a sermon. The first preacher they had, before there was any church organization, was John Koppejan of Oostburg, Wisconsin, who had been an elder in the Old Country among the Afgescheidenen, or Seceders, from the State Church. In Wisconsin he had started an independent church and was ordained by one of his elders.

As nearly all the Hollanders who had settled in Sayville had been brought up in the Reformed State Church in the Netherlands, they naturally were attracted to the Reformed Church in America, both having the same creed and polity. Here they found the daughter of the mother they had left behind. Seeing that they could not do effective work unless organized into a church, steps were taken to that end in view. The organization of the Reformed Church here, accordingly, took place on December 19, 1866, with thirty one members, the first ruling elders being John Westerlake, Sr. and John Hiddink, and the first deacons, Marinus Boot and John Otto. Dominie Louis Jongeneel from South Africa, who had already labored among them for sometime, was called as their pastor in December of that year. The installation services were held in the old school house of Sayville on April 3, 1867. Active measures now were taken to secure a church in which to worship; a building committee was appointed and the work vigorously pushed so that by their own exertions and by some outside help the present church edifice was dedicated on the 17th of November, 1867, Dominie Jongeneel labored here for nearly five years, until the summer of 1878.

The following year Dominie Gerrit van Emmerick, a lay preacher from Amsterdam, the Netherlands, then in New York City, was called, ordained and installed as pastor of this church. His pastoral services continued from June 1872 till the summer of 1886 - a period of 14 years. He was followed by Jean S. Crousaz, another lay candidate. He was licensed to preach by the North Classis of Long Island and ordained and installed in the pastorate in the latter part of 1887, and served the church for about two years. The church was then without a pastor until October, 1889, when Dr. J. C. Calkoen from South Africa ministered to its needs for nearly six months. In January, 1893, the writer of this sketch, then stationed at Clymer, New York, was invited to take charge of the pulpit and began his ministry in May of that year.

If the Dutch motto Eendracht maakt macht had been observed-that is if the Hollanders had been united from the beginning - we might have had a single strong church in West Sayville. But wherever Hollanders have settled in America, they have been religiously divided and so it was here. From the first some were unwilling to cast their lot with the Reformed Church. They stood aloof and, at the time when Dominie Willem Coenraad Wust of Lodi, New Jersey, made such a stir in the church because the word "Dutch" was dropped from its name, seceded, calling themselves "Dutch Reformed" and became Wust's followers. His followers and other elements later were organized into a Christian Reformed Church which was established more than twenty years ago. The first and only minister they have had was Dominie John de Vries who left them two years ago. At the time when a call was presented to him, he was a candidate for the ministry from the Theological School at Grand Rapids, Michigan. In this his first congregation he labored for nearly four years.

Thus I have briefly given you an outline of the history of Sayville and of the settling of the Hollanders there. They immigrated to the New World not for the sake of enjoying liberty of conscience, as so many of their countrymen did, but for the purpose of bettering their worldly fortunes. They had no leaders, as did the Hollanders who went West, such as Dominie H. P. Scholte, Dr. A. C. van Raalte, Dominie Seine Bolks, Dominie C. van der Meulen, Dominie Maarten Anne Ypma, and others. With their limited education these Dutch settlers did the best they could; and it is surprising that they steered their craft well in a land so strange to them in speech and manners. But in all this we note a higher guiding hand that had a hidden destiny in store for them to fulfill for themselves and their posterity on these American shores.

In conclusion I would say that although these Hollanders came without money or means they never suffered the hardships and privations incident to   so many of the new Dutch settlements in the West.   They always were able to earn some money, and by industry and economy make a decent living.   Able bodied men at present make from $1.50 to $ 2 a day.   Providence has blessed them and smiled upon them so they need not lack the necessaries of life.   May they and all the Hollanders who came as strangers to a strange land prove grateful to Him who led them to a land of plenty blessed with the fullest political and religious liberty.   May their descendants always acknowledge Him as the One who caused them to be born citizens of this great Republic.   We may well be proud of the fact that American citizenship is ours, whether by adoption or by birth.   Notwithstanding the privileges we are enjoying there is danger that posterity may forget God and His mercies; for the tendency of our times is materialistic. it requires special grace from on high not to be swallowed up by worldly mindedness, by pleasures and amusements so detrimental to the stability of the commonwealth, the higher interests of God's kingdom, and the soul's eternal welfare.   Cherishing a truly religious spirit, observing strictly the moral law, and copying the example of Jesus Christ will be our only safeguard,   So let it be.

Muster roll of the several Companies of the Burgher Corps of
New Amsterdam. 1653.

[Albany Records, VIII.]

1.
Captain   Arent van Hattem,
Sergeant,   David Provoost,
Corporal,   Claes Carstensen,
Lance Corporal,   Willem Pietersen,
Cadets, Claes Bordingh, Isaac Kip,
       Andries de Haes, Albert Coninck,

Privates.
Hage Bruynsen,
[Erasure.]
Jan Gerritsen, mason,
Hendrick Egberts,
Hans Stein,
Teunis Fredriks,
Andries Hopper,
Ary Jacobsen,
Harmen Bilderbeeck,
Jacob Bakker,
Thomas Lambertsen,
Geurt Coertsen,

3.
Lieutenant,   Paul L. van der Grist,
Sergeant,   Gerrit Loockermans,
Corporal,   Johannis Verbrugge,
Lance Corporal,   Conrad ten Eyck,
Cadets, Abr. Clock, Joris Woolsey,
       Isaac Foreest, Marcus Hendricks.

Privates.
Pieter Pietersen,
Andries Edwarts,
Cornelis Jans Seent,
Barent Jacobs Crol,
Auke Jansen,
Jacob Tys van Heide,
Wynand Gongelmans,
Stoffel Elbertsen,
Roelof Jansen Vouck,
Harmen Thunisz,
Cornelis Hendricksen,
Jacob van den Bos,
Dirck Jansen tot Loockermans,
Egbert Gerritsen,
Fredrick Hendricksen,
Carsten Malys.

2.
Ensign   Van Beeck,
Sergeant,   Arent Dircksen,
Corporal   Abr. de la Noy,
Lance Corporal,   Abr. Pietersen,
Cadets, Nicolaes Boot, Jan de Cuyper,
       Michl. Pouwelsen, Cors. Pietersen

Privates.
Hendrick Hendricksen,
Jan Hutsen,
Roelof Jansen,
Claes Hendricksen,
Andries Jochemsen,
Johannes Withart,
Abr. Martensen,
Pieter Loockermans,
Gerrit Gerritsen,
Andries de Kuyper,
Hendrick Gerritsen,
Willem Albertsen,
Lucas Andriessen,
Bernard Wessels,
Adam Roelantsen,

4.
Senior Sergeant,   Daniel Lush, [Litschoe?]
Corporal,   Pieter van Naerden,
Lance Corporal,   Lodewyck Pots,
Cadets, J. de Peyster, Egbert Woutersen,
       Math. de Vos, Anthony de Moor,

Privates.
Pieter Jacobsen,
Egbert van Borsum,
Albert Jansen,
Jan Dircksen,
Claes Tysen Cuyper,
Cornelis Willemsen,
Claes van Elsland,
Jacob Vis,
Harman Rutgers,
Cornelis Jansen Coelen,
Adriaen Blommaert,
Jan Peeck,
Lowris Cornelissen,

List of Patents issued by the Dutch Government from 1630 to 1664,
rendered as complete as the Books of Patents and Town Records now admit.

Names of Patentees.	Description of Grant.	Location of Grant.	Date of Patent.
Paauw, Michel	Hobocan Hacking,	Pavonia,	13 July, 1630.
Godyn, Samuel	An Indian tract,	Cape Hinlopen,	15 " "
Paauw, Michel	" "	Staten Island	10 Aug. "
" "	" "	Ahasimus,	22 Nov. "
Goodyn and Blommaert	" "	Cape May,	3 June, 1631.
Van Rensselaer, Kiliaen	" E. side N.R.	Rensselaerswyck,	6 Aug. "
" "	" W. " "	"	13 " "
West India Company,	The Sicajoock flatt,	Connecticut,	8 June, 1633.
" " "	Armenveruis,	South River,	8 " "
Van Curler, Jacob	3 Flatts,	Castateeuw, (a)	16 " 1636.
Hudde, Andries et al.	1 "	Kaskuteusuhane, (a)	16 " "
Van Twiller, Wouter	1 "	(a)	16 July, "
Jans, Roeloff and Anatje	31 morgens,	Manhattans, (b)	
Van Rensselaer,Kiliaen	An Indian tract,	Papskeena,	13 April, 1637.
Van Twiller, Wouter	Pagganck,	Now Governor's Island	16 June "
Rapalje, George	An Indian tract,	Wallabout,	16 " "
Van Twiller, Wouter	2 Islands,	Hellgat,	16 July, "
Bronck, Jonas	The Ranaque tract,	North of Haerlem,	"
Hudde, Andries	A plantation,	Behind Corlears Hook,	20 " 1638.
West India Company,	An Indian tract,	Bet. B'klen & Mespath,	1 Aug. "
" " "	" " "	From Rockaway to)	15 Jan'y, 1639.
		Mart. Gerritsen's Bay)	
Jansen van Salee, Anth.	10 morgens,	Long Island,	1 Aug. "
West India Company,	Hiskeshick,	Manhattans,	3 " "
Hall, Thomas and)	Deutel bay,	"	15 Nov. "
Holmes, George)			
Bescher, Thomas	300 paces sq.,	Marreckkawick,(c)	28 " "
De Truy, Philip	Land,	Smith's valley, Manhat.	22 May, 1640.
Lubbertsen, Fredrick	"	Marrekkawick, (B'klen)	27 " "
Van Linden, Pieter	"	Manhattans,	2 Aug. "
Rycken, Abram	"	Long Island,	8 " "
Montfoort, Pieter	"	" "	29 May, 1641.
" Jan	"	" "	29 " "
Baxter, Geo. et al.	"	Manhattans,	29 Aug. "
Cornelisen, Laurens	25 morgens,	"	7 Sept. "
Mol, Lamb't Huybertsz.	25 "	Rinnegaconck,(d)	7 " "
Nederhorst, the Heer	A Colonie,	West side of the Hudson	1641
Loockermans, Govert	Land,	Wolferts v'ly B'klen	26 Mar. 1642
		fer.	
" "	A house and lot,	Manhattans,	26 " "
Jansen, Tymen	Land,	Mespath kill,	"
Doughty, Rev. Frs.	A Colonie,	"	28 Mar. "
Cool, Corn. Lamberts	25 morgens,	Gowanus	5 April, "
Melyn, Cornelis	The major part of	Staten Island,	19 June, "
Manje, Jan	20 morgens,	Breukelen,	11 Sept. "
Van Schouw, Claes Corn.	Land,	Long Island,	14 Nov. "
Hall, Thomas	"	Manhattans,	20 " "
Ryken, Abram et al.	A lot	New Amsterdam,	8 April, 1643
Kip, Hend'k Hendricks	"	"	28 " "
Jorissen, Borger	"	"	28 " "
Hooglandt, Corn's Dirck	2 morgens,	Breukelen,	28 " "
Krygier, Martin	A lot,	New Amsterdam,	18 May, "
Schepmoes, J. Jansz.	"	"	18 " "
Allerton, Isaac	"	"	2 June, "
Provoost, David	"	"	2 " "
Huygen, Jan	"	"	6 " "
Italiaen, Petr. Cesar	Tobacco plantation,	Long Island	17 " "
Van Twiller, Wouter	Red Hook,	"	22 " "
Duycking,Ev't V. Borcken	A lot,	Manhattans,	22 " "

(a) Now Flatlands, L.I.
(b) This is the celebrated Annetje Jans tract, now in possession of Trinity Church, New Yor
It was confirmed to the widow and heirs of Dom. Bogardus, 4 July, 1654.
(c) Now Brooklyn
(d) Described as situated on Manhattan Island, south of the farm of Hans Hansen.

Names of Patentees.	Description of Grant.	Location of Grant.	Date of Patent.
Verplanck, Abram	A lot,	New Amsterdam,	3 July, 1643.
Laurens, Chr.	22 morgens,	North River bay,	3 " "
Stevensen, Jan	a lot,	New Amsterdam,	3 " "
Jansen, Tymen	Land,	Manhattan Island,	3 " "
Jorissen, Borger	30 morgens,	Mespath kill,	3 " "
Couwenhoven, J.W. van	10 "	Long Island	3 " "
Hudde, Andries	A lot,	New Amsterdam	6 " "
Schepmoes, J. Jansz.	"	"	6 " "
Haes, Roeloff Jansz.	"	"	6 " "
Baxter, Geo.	25 morgens,	Long Island,	6 " "
Briel, Toussaint	11 "	Manhattans,	6 " "
Trogmorton, John	Vreedland,	Westchester	6 " "
Geraerdy, Philip	A lot,	New Amsterdam	13 " "
Teunissen, Anna	"	"	13 " "
Aertsen Rutger	"	"	13 " "
Van Seyl, Rutg. Arent	"	"	13 " "
Domingo, Anthonie	5 morgens,	Manhattans,	13 " "
Anthony, wid. of Jochem	4 "	"	13 " "
Jansen, Tymen	A lot	Long Island	13 " "
Volckertsen, Cornelis	Double lot	New Amsterdam	13 " "
Sandersen, Thomas	A lot,	"	13 " "
Britnel, Richard	25 morgens,	Mespath kill,	28 " "
Rolantsen, Adam	A lot,	New Amsterdam,	7 Aug. "
Couwenhoven, Pieter van	"	"	7 " "
Tomassen, Wm.	"	"	7 " "
Montfort, Peter	Tobacco plantation,	Long Island,	17 " "
Van Steenwyck,Abr. Jacobs.	A lot,	New Amsterdam,	14 Nov. "
Montfort, Jan	28 morgens	"	1 Dec. "
Nyssen, Teunis	A lot,	"	5 Dec. "
Manuel, trump'tr (fr. neg.)	9 morgens,	Manhattans,	12 " "
Marycke (free negress)	3 "	"	12 " "
Jorissen, Borger	A lot,	New Amsterdam,	20 Jan'y, 1644
Jansen, Hend'k (tailor)	Double lot,	"	20 " "
Jonas, Tryntie	A lot,	Manhattans,	Feb. "
Jans, Tryntie	"	"	15 April, "
Couwenhoven, Pieter	"	"	25 " "
Dam, Jan Jansen	"	"	25 " "
Vigne, Adrian	Double lot,	"	25 " "
Verplanck, Abram	A lot,	"	25 " "
Melyn, Cornelis	Double lot,	"	28 " "
Geraerdy, Philip	A lot,	New Amsterdam	24 May, "
Op Dyck, Guysbert	Conyen Island,	In the bay,	24 May, "
Marschan, Michel	A lot,	New Amsterdam,	" "
Van Naerdin, Claes Jansz.	A double lot,	"	" "
Vincent, Ariaen	"	"	1 June, "
Ruyter, Claes Janz.	"	"	2 " "
Huygen, Jan	A lot,	"	6 " "
Smith, Hend'k Jansz.	"	"	13 " "
Van Tienhoven, Corns.	12 morgens,	"	14 " "
Van der Grist, P. Leend.	A lot,	"	19 July, "
Broen, Thomas	"	"	25 Aug. "
Schepmoes, J. Jansen	"	"	8 Sept. "
Van Jorcum, Pieter Jansz.	"	"	8 " "
Cornelissen, Pieter	"	"	8 " "
Roy, Jacob Jacobsz.	"	"	9 " "
Heemstede, town of	A Township,	Long Island,	16 Nov. "
DeWitt, Jan (the miller)	A lot,	New Amsterdam	15 Dec. "
Congo, Simon(free neg.)	4 morgens,	Manhattans,	15 " "
Santonee, Ptr. (")	3 "	"	15 " "
D'Angola, Gratio(")	5 "	"	15 " "
Manuel, Groot. (")	6 "	"	21 " "
Cleyn, Antonio (")	3 "	"	30 " "
D'Angola, Paulo (")	3 "	"	30 " "

Names of Patentees.	Description of Grant.	Location of Grant.	Date of Patent.
Groesens, Cornelis	A Lot,	New Amsterdam,	10 Jan'y, 1645
Volckertsen, Dirck	25 morgens,	Mespath,	3 April, "
Couwenhoven,J.Wolf.van	1 lot,	New Amsterdam,	18 May, "
Cornelissen, Jan	2 "	"	23 June, "
Pietersen, Gilles	1 "	"	4 July, "
Jan, Teunis (sailmaker)	1 "	"	4 " "
Willett, Thomas	1 "	"	4 " "
Van Naarden,Teunis T.	1 "	"	4 " "
Smith, Richd. Senr.	1 "	"	4 " "
Van Tienhoven,	100 morgens	Manhattans island,	-- " "
Snediker, Jan	1 double lot,	"	-- " "
Bout, Jan Evertsen	A piece of land,	Gowanus kill,	6 " "
Breser, Henry	16 morgens,	Long Island,	4 Sept. "
Lubbertsen, Frederick	15 morgens,	Manhattans,	4 " "
Van Cortland Ol. Stev. (Commis.)	1 lot,	"	5 " "
Carstensen, Claes	29 morgens,	Long Island,	5 " "
Snediker, Jan	1 lot,	Manhattans,	5 " "
Fradel, Juriaen	69 morgens,	Long Island,	5 " "
De Foreest, Isaac	A lot,	Manhattans,	5 " "
Van Alkmaer, Ariaen Pieters	"	New Amsterdam,	7 " "
West India Company,	An Indian tract,	Now, New Utrecht,	10 " "
Hudde, Andries	37 morgens,	Breukelen,	12 Sept. 1645.
Sandersen, Thomas	A lot,	Manhattans,	14 " "
Van Dincklage, Lubbert	"	"	22 " "
Aerden, Leendert	"	New Amsterdam,	22 " "
Van Naerden, Claes Jans.	21 morgens,	Breukelen,	30 " "
Peers, Hendrick	A lot,	Manhattans,	30 " "
Calder, Jochem	"	"	30 " "
Flushing, Town of	A township	Long Island,	19 Oct. "
Andriessen, Pieter	Dominie's Hook	Manhattans,	19 " "
" "	A lot,	Near the Tavern,N.A.	19 " "
Aerden, Leendert	Bylevelt's Bouwerie (a)	Behind Corlear's Hook	19 " "
Bridel, Toussaint	11 morgens,	Manhattans,	19 " "
Manuel, Groot (negro)	4 "	"	19 " "
Marrel, Edouard	11 "	West of Corlear's Hook,	22 " "
" "	A lot,	Manhattans,	3 Nov. "
Lodewyck, Hans	14 morgens,	"	3 " "
Pennoyer, Robert	89 "	Gravesend,	29 " "
Couwenhoven,J.W. van	A lot	Behind the Tavern,N.A.	12 Dec. "
Dircksen, Cornelis	12 morgens,	Long Island	13 " "
Swits, Cornelis Claesz.	Bowerie No. 5, 25 mor.	Manhattans,	13 " "
Gravesend, Town of	A township	Long Island	19 " "
Van der Donck, Adriaen	An Indian tract,	Nepperhaem or Yonkers	1646.
West India Company,	"	Schuylkill,	
Haes, Roeloff Jansz.	A lot,	Manhattans,	1 Feb. "
Jansen, Roeloff	"	"	2 " "
Cornelissen, Pieter	27 morgens	Marrekkawick, (B'kelen)	8 " "
Ryken, Abram	A lot,	Manhattans,	14 " "
Van Oldenborgh, Ger. J.	46 morgens,	Pannebacker's Bou.	17 " "
Cornelissen, Willem	25 "	Marrekkawick, L.I.	19 " "
Van Rosum, Huych Aerts.	90 "	"	22 " "
Dam, Jan Jansen	20 "	Kalckhoeck Manh. Is'd	15 Mar. "
Hartgers, Pieter	A lot,	New Amsterdam,	17 " "
Couwenhoven, P.W. van	"	"	17 " "
Dircksen, Joris	18 morgens	Marrekkawick, L.I.	23 " "
Van der Linden, Pieter	A lot,	New Amsterdam,	23 " "
Lambertsen, Reyer	57 morgens,	Marrekkawick, L.I.	23 " "
Roy, Jacob Jacobs.	Constaples Hoeck,	Achter Kul,	
Van Tienhoven, Cornelis	A lot,	Manhattans,	27 " "
Holmes, George	"	"	23 April, "
Jansen, Roeloff	"	New Amsterdam,	11 May, "
Van der Beeke,	"	"	12 " "
Claessen, Sybout	"	"	12 " "
Underhill, Capt. John	Mattelaer's Island,	Amersfoort,	14 " "
Claessen, Sybout	15 morgens,	Manhattans,	5 June, "
Cornell, Thomas	Cornell's neck,	Westchester,	26 " "
Evertsen, Wessell	A lot,	New Amsterdam,	2 July, "
Van der Wel, Laur. Corns.	Double lot	Smith's valley,	2 " "

(a) Sold in 1663 to General Stuyvesant, and called, Myn Heer Stuyvesant's Bouwerie.

Names of Patentees.	Description of Grant.	Location of Grant.	Date of Patent.
Planck, Abr. et al.	What lands they please,	South River,	10 Aug. 1646.
Jansen, Matys	50 morgens,	Papperimemin (Manhats)	18 " "
De Foreest, Isaac	A lot,	New Amsterdam,	22 " "
Van Slyck, Corns. Anth.	Katskill,	Katskill,	22 " "
Mott, Adam	25 morgens,	Mespath kill,	23 " "
Pauluszen, Michel	A lot	New Amsterdam,	15 Sept. "
Cornelisen, Pieter	"	"	24 Oct. "
Douwman, Gerrit			29 Nov. "
Hendricksen, Gerrit	Scouts bouwerie 25 m.	Manhattans,	6 Dec. "
Lubbertsen, Fredrick	A lot,	New Amsterdam	21 Jan'y, 1647
Baxter, Geo. et al.	Canarissee,	Long Island	21 " "
Pauluszen, Michel	A lot,	Manhattans,	21 " "
Pietersen, Corns.	"	"	21 " "
Kierstede, Surg'n. Hans			21 " "
Heymanse, Paul	"	"	3 Feb. "
Brouwer, Adam	"	"	7 " "
Jansen, Evert		"	8 " "
D'Angola, Anna (negress)	3 morgens,		8 " "
Bout, Jan Everts	A lot,	"	19 " "
Jansen, Pieter et al.	74 morgens,	Montagne's bay Manhat.	11 Mar. "
Couwenhoven, G.W. van	19 "	Reckaweck, L.I.	11 " "
Buller, Robert	A lot,	Manhattans,	12 " "
Willemsen, Cornelis	22 morgens,	Mespath,	12 " "
Baxter, Thomas	A lot,	Manhattans,	12 " "
Van der Linden, P.	"	"	12 " "
Stevensen, Oloff	30 morgens,	Sapokanickan, M.I.	12 " "
Noorman, Laurs. Ptsn.	A lot	Manhattans,	12 " "
Hansen, Hans	A farm	"	13 " "
Gerritsen, Cosyn	34 morgens and 1 lot	Sapokanickan, M.I.	13 " "
Van Elslandt, Claes	12 " " "	"	13 " "
Planck, Abram	A lot,	Manhattans,	14 " "
Van Tienhoven, Corns.	A plantation	Breukelen,	15 " "
Van Bogaert, Harm. M.	A lot,	Manhattans,	16 " "
Monfoort, Jan	"	"	16 " "
" , Pieter	"	"	16 " "
Van Valkenburgh, Lamb't	"	"	16 " "
Rapelje, Joris	"	"	18 " "
Backer, Claes Jansen	"	"	18 " "
Stille, Corns. Jacobs.	28 morgens,	"	18 " "
Van Ditmarsen, Jan Jans.	29 "		23 " "
Noorman, Claes Jansz.	50 "	West side North River	25 " "
Francisco, (negro)	A piece of land,	" "	25 " "
Cornelissen, Wm.	A lot,	" "	25 " "
Congo, Anthony (negro)	A piece of land,	Manhattans,	26 " "
Bastiaen, (")	" "	"	26 " "
Jan, (")			26 " "
Lauressen, Pieter	A lot	"	28 " "
Nysen, Teunis	"	"	28 " "
Jansen, Rem.		"	29 " "
Borsum, Jan Pietersen	4 morgens	Long Island	29 " "
Hansen, Hans	200 "	Mespath,	30 " "
Haes, Jan	38 "	Reckaweck, L.I.	2 April "
Smeeman, Harman	23 "	Manhattans,	2 " "
Nysen, Teunis	A plantation		3 " "
Van Campen, Pieter	3 morgens,		8 " "
Pietersen, Jochem	A lot	"	10 " "
Kierstede, Jochem	"	"	12 " "
Van Alemaer, Ariaen Ptsn	A plantation	Sapokanekan, (Manhatt)	13 " "
Schage, W. Cornelissen	A lot	New Amsterdam,	15 " "
Cray, Teunis	"	"	15 " "
Blanck, Juriaen		"	15 " "
Pierse, Henry	A plantation,	Manhattans,	15 " "
Schoonmaker, C. Teunis	A lot,	"	15 " "
Italiaen, Peter Cesar	220 rods,	Long Island	1 May "
Montfort, Peter	220 "	Near Brooklyn,	1 " "
" Widow	190 " sq.	" "	1 " "
La Montagne, Jan	100 morgens,	Manhattans,	9 " "
Woutersen, Egbert	Apopcalyck,	Near Gamoenepaen,	10 " "
Adriaensen, Maryn	A plantation,	Awiehaken,	11 " "
Heermans, Augustine	4 lots,	New Amsterdam,	15 " "
Claesen, Sybout	"	"	15 " "
Forbes, John	65 morgens	L. Island on East Riv.	15 " "

Names of Patentees.	Description of Grant.	Location of Grant.	Date of Patent.
De Foreest, Isaac	50 Morgens,	Manhattans,	15 April, 1647.
Hall, Thomas	A lot,	"	15 " "
Daniel, ---	1 morgen,	"	15 " "
Huybertsen, Sergeant	A lot,	"	16 " "
Linde, Pieter	"	"	12 Nov. "
Jansen, Maritie	"	"	17 May, 1648.
Van der Veer, P. Corns	"	"	17 " "
Van der Douck, Adriaen	A plantation,	Near Mespath, L.I.	17 " "
Van Rensselaer, Patroon	An Indian tract,	Paponikuck,	4 Sept. "
Stickland, Lieut. John	200 morgens,	Jerusalem, Hempstead	23 Dec. "
Roy, Jacob Jacobs.	A lot,	New Amsterdam,	15 April, 1649.
Van Rensselaer, Patroon	An Indian tract,	Katskill,	19 " "
Jansen, H'k van Utrecht	A lot,	New Amsterdam,	20 " "
Karstensen, Claes	"	"	3 May, "
Van der Grist, P.L.	"	"	14 " "
Van Rensselaer, Patroon	An Indian tract,	Claverack,	27 " "
Andriessen, Juriaen	A lot,	New Amsterdam,	6 June, "
West India Company,	An Indian tract,	Wechquaesqueeck,	14 July, "
Stuyvesant, Balthazar	A lot,	New Amsterdam,	20 " "
" Nicolas Wm.	"	"	20 " "
Varrevanger, J. Hendricks	"	"	
Megapolensis, Rev. John	"	"	24 April, 1650.
Duycking, Evert	"	"	30 " "
Van Nes, Dirck	"	"	23 May, "
Michelsen, Jan	"	Beverwyck,	23 " "
Martyn, Jan	"	New Amsterdam,	26 July, "
Kuyter, Jochem Pietersz	A plantation.	Manhattans, (a)	14 Nov. "
Ten Eyck, Coenraet	A lot,	New Amsterdam,	4 Jan'y, 1651
Bridel, Toussaint	"	"	10 " "
De Spanjie,	"	"	18 " "
Jansen, Fredrick	"	"	10 Mar. "
Heermans, Augustyn	An Indian tract,	Raritans,	28 " "
La Montague, Joannes	A lot,	New Amsterdam	22 April 1651.
Newton, Brian	"	"	27 " "
Van Tienhoven, Cornelis	"	"	20 Sept. "
Bloemmaert, Adriaen	"	"	20 " "
Loockermans, Govert	"	"	20 " "
De Vos, Mattys	"	"	20 " "
Ffyn, Capt. Frs.	Hog Island,	Near Hellegat,	20 " "
Van Werckhoven, Corns.	2 colonies,	Nyack; Nevesings	7 Nov. "
Church and Sch'ls of Midwout,	14 lots,	Midwout,	
Jacobsen, Rutger	A lot,	Beverwyck,	23 April, 1652
Van Schaick, Goosen G.	"	"	23 " "
De Hooges, Anthonie	"	"	23 " "
Teunissen, Cornelis	"	"	23 " "
Herbertsen, Andries	"	"	23 " "
Jansen, Dirck	"	"	23 " "
Andriessen, Arent	"	"	23 " "
Jansen, Volckert	"	"	23 " "
Gerritsen, Albert	"	"	23 " "
Adriaensen, Jacob	"	"	23 " "
Teller, Willem	"	"	23 " "
Bogardus, Annetje	"	"	23 " "
Jacobsen, Teunis	"	"	23 " "
Adriaensen, Rut	"	"	23 " "
Pieters, Albert	"	New Amsterdam,	1 July "
Schermerhoorn, Jacob Jansz.	"	Beverwyck,	9 Nov. "
Steendam, Jacob et al.	A plantation,	Amersfoort,	12 " "
Bogardus, Annetje Jans	65 morgens,	Mespath, (b)	26 " "
Midwout, town of	Township,	Long Island	
Hallet, Wm.	80 morgens,	"	1 Dec. "

(a) Schorrakyn, the Indian name for a lot of land belonging to Jochem Pietersen Kuyter on Manhattan Island - called in Dutch Zegendal, "bounded south by Wm. Beekman's lot; at the end Johannes La Montagne to the first rock in a north course to the great kill to the east, on the North River a grass valley, three or four morgens large."
(b) This tract (Dominie's Hook) has been recently purchased for Union College, Schenectady.

Names of Patentees.	Description of Grant.	Location of Grant.	Date of Patent.
Pietersen, Claes	A lot,	Fort Casimir,	6 Dec. 1652.
Van Hasselt, Hend'k Pieters.	"	New Amsterdam,	28 Jan'y, 1653.
Hendricksen, Claes	"	"	2 Feb. "
Drisius, Rev. Samuel	"	"	24 " "
Bicker, Gerrit	25 morgens,	Midwout,	25 " "
Backer, Jochem	A lot	Beverwyck,	23 April, "
Loockermans, Pieter	"	"	7 July, "
Kierstede, Hans	"	"	18 " "
Shrick, Paulus	2 morgens,	The Kolck, New Am.	7 Oct. "
Cray, Teunis	37 "	Near Hellegat, L.I.	25 " "
Elbertsen, Ryer	A lot,	Beverwyck,	25 " "
Lourenzen, Laurens	"	"	25 " "
Kettelhuyn, Jochem	"	"	25 " "
Van Embden, Evert Jansz.	"	"	25 " "
Jacobsen, Casper,	"	"	25 " "
Reyckersen, Michel	"	"	25 " "
Andriessen, Hendrick	"	"	25 " "
Verbeck, Jan	"	"	25 " "
Jansen, Thomas	"	"	25 " "
De Vos, Andries	A lot of woodland,	"	25 " "
Sandersen, Thomas	2 lots,	"	25 " "
Adriaensen, Rut	A lot,	"	25 " "
Appel van Leyden, Adr. Jansz.	2 lots,	"	25 " "
Schermerhoorn, Jacob Jansz.	"	"	25 " "
Labadie, Jan	A lot	"	25 " "
Jansen, Laurens	"	"	25 " "
Staets, Cant. Abram	"	"	25 " "
Sibbinck, Jacob Hendrick	"	"	25 " "
Klomp, Jacob Symonsz.	"	"	25 " "
Bruynsen, Hage	"	"	25 " "
Van Hoesen, Jan Frs.	"	"	25 " "
Pietersen, Gillis	"	"	25 " "
Van Bronswyck, P. Jansz.	25 morgens,	Katskill,	25 " "
Gerardy, Philip	25 "	Long Island,	2 Nov. "
" , Jean	20 "	Green Hook. L.I.	5 " "
Chambers, Thomas	38 "	Esopus	8 " "
Van Bronswyck, P. Jansz.	6 "	Katskill,	16 " "
Huybertsen, Adriaen	A lot,	At the Ferry, L.I.	12 " "
Jansen, Michel	Schreyer's Hook,	Manhattans,	
" Lieven	A plantation,	Long Island,	26 Feb. 1654.
Bogardus, Annetje Jans	42 morgens,	"	7 Mar. "
Staets, Capt. Abram	Cickhekawick,	North of Claverack,	17 " "
Philipsen, Leendert	A lot,	Beverwyck,	24 " "
Marcelis, Hendrick	"	"	24 " "
Pietersen, Gillis	"	"	14 April, "
Van Ruyven, Cornelis	"	New Amsterdam	16 " "
Van Dyck, Hendrick	"	"	11 May, "
Van der Grist, P. Leenderts.	"	"	11 " "
Van Brugge, Carel	"	"	22 " "
Van Tienhoven, Rachel	"	"	22 " "
" " Cornelis	"	"	22 " "
De Sille, Nicasius	"	"	22 " "
Van Hattem, Arent	A plantation,	Midwout,	4 June, "
Zieken, Dirck	"	Near Gamoenepaen,	16 " "
Coen, Adriaen Dircksen	16 morgens,	Middelburgh, L.I.	18 " "
Carpenel, Jan Jacobsen	25 morgens	"	22 " "
Coen, Adriaen Dircksen	25 "	" "	22 " "
Monfoort, Jan	A lot,	New Amsterdam,	28 " "
Syboutsen, Hark	21 morgens,	Middelburgh, L.I.	2 July, "
Drisius, Rev. Samuel	A plantation	Manhattans,	2 " "
Van Borsum, Egbert	2 lots,	Breukelen,	18 " "
Monfoort, Jan	"	New Amsterdam	28 " "
Gerritsen, Wynout	A lot,	Beverwyck,	29 Aug. "
Westphael, Juriaen	32-1/2 morgens,	Esopus,	
Swaen, Jan	A lot,	New Amsterdam,	23 Oct. "

Names of Patentees.	Description of Grant.	Location of Grant.	Date of Patent.
Walingen, Jacob (Van Hoorn)	25 morgens,	Behind Kill van Kul,(a)	23 Oct. 1654.
Huybertsen, Adriaen	22 "	Mespath,	14 Nov. "
Dircksen, Luycas	16 "	"	21 " "
Jansen, Michel	26-1/3 "	Behind Kill van Kul,	27 " "
Bakker, Claes Jansen	40 "	"	27 " "
Luby, Sergeant Jacob	25 "	Mespath,	30 " "
Bredenbent, William	A lot,	New Amsterdam,	1 Dec. "
Buys, Jan Cornelissen	25 morgens,	Behind Kill van Kul,	4 " "
Lubbertsen, Jan	25 "	" " " "	5 " "
Van Immen, Jan Gerrits	25 "	" " " "	5 " "
Schoonmaker, Jan Corns.	25 "	" " " "	5 " "
Pietersen, Gerrit	25 "	" " " "	5 " "
Gysbertsen, Lubbert	50 "	" " " "	5 " "
Crynnen, Jan Cornelisen	25 "	" " " "	5 " "
Lubbertsen, Gysbert	25 "	" " " "	5 " "
Van Schalckwyk, H'k J.	25 "	" " " "	5 " "
Leydecker, Reyck	25 "	Mespath,	10 " "
Jansen, Roeloff	25 "	"	10 " "
Swaen, Jan	25 "	"	15 " "
Smith, Ensign Dirck	54 "	"	15 " "
Appel van Leyden, Ad.J.	A lot for an inn,	Beverwyck,	16 " "
Stoutenbergh, Pieter	6 morgens	Long Island	
Clock, Abram Martens	A lot,	New Amsterdam,	26 Aug. 1655.
Van der Donck, Cornelis	Muscoote,	North end of Manhattans,	26 " "
De Foreest, Isaac	27 morgens,	Midwout,	1 Dec. "
Matthys, Anthony, (fr. neg.)	A lot,	Manhattans,	"
Ffyn, Capt. Frs.	26 morgens,	Long Island,	26 Feb. 1656.
Gemeco, (Rustdorp)	Township	"	21 Mar. "
DeSille, Nicasius	126 morgens,	Mespath,	27 " "
" "	An Island,	Arnhem,	27 " "
Middelburgh, (Newtown)	Township,	Long Island,	12 April "
Broen, Thomas	2096 rods,	Fort Casimir,	12 " "
Rudolphus, Pieter	A lot,	New Amsterdam,	18 May, "
Bakker, Nicolas Jansz.	"	"	18 " "
Cock, Jochem Gerrits	1 morgen	Breukelen,	27 " "
Schuyler, Ph. Pietersen	2 lots,	Beverwyck,	16 June, "
Coen, Adriaen Dircks	A lot,	New Amsterdam	19 " "
Draper, Hans	"	"	20 " "
Edsal, Samuel	"	"	20 " "
Beekman, Willem	"	"	20 " "
Kip, Isaack	"	"	21 " "
" Jacob	"	"	21 " "
Couwenhoven, J.W. van	The old Church and lot	"	30 " "
Catyou, Jan	25 morgens,	Mespath	21 Aug. "
Van Yveren, H'K Jans	25 "	L.I. near Hellegat,	25 " "
DeHinse, Surgeon Jacob	2 lots,	Fort Casimir,	25 " "
Picolet, Jan	3 morgens,	"	1 Sept. "
Ringoa, Philip Jansz.	A lot,	"	12 " "
Groenenburgh, Constan.	"	"	13 " "
Van Bronswyck, Hans Alb.	"	"	13 " "
DeBoer, H'k Jansen	"	New Amsterdam,	19 " "
Van Struckhousen, J. Hen.	"	Fort Casimir,	22 " "
Davits, Christoffel	36 morgens,	Esopus,	25 " "
Kierstede, Hans	A lot,	New Amsterdam,	25 Oct. "
Ilpendam, Adriaen Jansz	" "	Beverwyck,	28 " "
Abrams, Mattheus			
DeHaes, wid. of Roeloff	A plantation,	Fort Casimir,	28 " "
Jansen, Reyn	A lot	Beverwyck,	16 Nov. "
Hudde, Andries	"	Fort Casimir,	30 " "
Boyer, Alexander	24 morgens,	"	30 " "
Loockermans, Govert	Water lot,	New Amsterdam	21 Dec. "
Clock, Abram Martens	" "	New Amsterdam	21 " "
Winkelhoeck, Pieter J.	25 morgens,	Mespath,	28 " "
Bernard, Nicolaes,	A lot,	New Amsterdam	Jan'y, 1657
Dircksen, Luycas	"	Fort Casimir,	10 Feb. "
Mol, Rver Lammersen	"	"	20 " "
Van Swel, Barent Jansz.	"	"	20 " "
Harmans, Pieter	Plantation and lot,		24 " "

(a) The patents behind the Kill van Kul, granted in 1654, constitute the present town of Bergen, N.J.

Names of Patentees.	Description of Grant.	Location of Grant.	Date of Patent.
Laurensen, Pieter	Plantation and lot,	Fort Casimir,	28 Feb. 1657.
Dominicus, Reynier	A lot,	"	(a)30 " "
Ebel, Pieter	9 morgens,	"_	(a)30 " "
Steenwyck, Cornelis	A lot,	"	(a)30 " "
Gerritse, Jan	"	"	(a)30 " "
Crabbe, Jacob	16 morgens,	"	(a)30 " "
Leendertsen, Sanders	A lot,	"	1 Mar. "
Taillera, Wm.	"	"	1 " "
DeLaat, Johan.(wid. Hulter)	500 morgens,	Esopus	27 " "
Provoost, Margrietje	25 "	Amersfoort,	1 June, "
Eeckhoff, Jan	a lot,	Fort Casimir,	17 " "
Andriessen, Jan	"	"	17 " "
's Gaggen, Jan	40 morgens,	"	20 " "
Barentsen, Christn.	A lot,	New Amsterdam.	1 Aug. "
Young, Hans	"	Breukelen,	25 " "
Utrecht, town of New	130 morgens,	Near Conyen Island	27 " "
Laurentsen, Pieter	A lot,	Fort Casimir,(N. Amstel)	3 " "
Hendricksen, Claes	2 lots,	Beverwyck,	25 Sept. "
DeSille, Nicasius	"	New Amsterdam,	5 Dec. "
Van Dyck, Hendrick	A lot	"	12 Dec. "
DeSille, Nicasius	"	"	19 " "
Duycking, Evert	33 morgens,	Midwout,	
Megapolensis, Rev. J.	32 "	"	
Philipsen, Frederick	A lot,	New Amsterdam,	9 Feb. 1658
Jacobsen, Pieter	"	Beverwyck,	23 " "
Steelman, Jan Hendricks	34 morgens,	Doughty farm,(Mespath)	25 " "
Van Rensselaer, Jeremias	A lot,	Beverwyck,	25 " "
Glen, Sander Leenderts,	"	"	13 July "
Cornelissen, Guilliam	A plantation,	Midwout,	9 Aug. "
Couwenhoven, G.W. van	Hudde's flatts,	Amersfoort,	24 " "
Schuyler, Phil. Pietersen	A lot,	Beverwyck,	10 Sept. "
Barentsen, Heirs of Bruyn	"	Breukelen,	4 Oct. "
Meersen, Pieter	"	Beverwyck,	31 " "
Chambers, Thomas	"	"	8 Nov. "
Van Langedyck, J. Jansen	"	New Amsterdam,	2 Dec. "
Angola, Domingo (fr. neg.)	2 lots,	"	"
Claes, de Neger (fr. neg.)	A lot	"	"
Assento, (fr. neg.)	"	"	"
Tamboer, Pieter (fr. neg.)	"	"	"
Cartagena, Francisco (fr. neg.)	"	"	"
DeRoos, Gr't Manuel (fr. neg.)	2 lots,	"	1659.
Santonie, Christoffel (fr. neg.)	A lot,	"	"
Sanders, Manuel (fr. neg.)	2 lots,	"	"
Antonys, Wm. (fr. neg.)	1 lot	"	"
Pieters, Solomon "	"	"	"
Angola, Assento " "	"	"	"
Pieter, Luycas " "	"	"	"
Antonys, Antony " "	"	"	"
Francisco, " "	"	"	"
Jansen, Volckert et al.	A plantation	Fort Orange	31 Mar. "
Andriessen, --	"	"	19 " "
Daniels, Gustavus	A lot,	Midwout,	21 " "

(a) Thus in the original.

Names of Patentees.	Description of Grant.	Location of Grant.	Date of Patent.
Van Curler, Arent	A plantation,	Beverwyck	23 Mar. 1659.
Loockermans, Gov. et al.		Mattinecong, Long Isl'd	23 " "
Van Nes, Cornelis	50 morgens,	Amersfoort,	23 May, "
Hartgers, Pieter	2 lots,	Beverwyck,	1 Sept. "
Daretha, Jan	A lot,	"	5 Feb. 1660
Jacobsen, Pieter	"	"	23 " "
Provoost, Margaretje	20 morgens	Midwout,	9 May, "
Andriessen, Andries	A lot,	New Amsterdam,	11 July, "
Cornelissen, Albert	"	"	13 " "
Mees, Peter	"	Beverwyck,	17 Aug. "
Martense, Jan	10 morgens	Amersfoort,	20 " "
Teunissen, Cornelis	25 "	"	
Benim, Evert	28 "		
Meyer, Pieter	A plantation,	Altona,	18 Sept. "
Jans, widow Elskie,	A lot,	New Amsterdam,	19 Oct. "
Martyn, Jan,		Ferry, Long Island	19 " "
Marten, Roeloff	23 morgens,	Amersfoort,	29 Jan'y, 1661
Swartwout, Thomas	58 "	Midwout,	7 Mar. "
Van Aecken, Jan Costers	A lot,	Beverwyck,	7 " "
Tomassen, Jan	2 lots,	"	10 " "
Jacobsen, Rutger et al.	Pachnachkillick Isl'd	Near Beverwyck,	10 " "
Jansen, Cornelis	60 morgens,	Midwout,	12 " "
Andriessen, Pieter	A lot,	New Amsterdam,	14 " "
Bushwyck, town of	Township	Long Island	14 " "
Jacobsen, Rutger	Constable's Island	Beverwyck,	19 " "
Jansen, Paulus	A plantation,	Altona,	7 April, "
Van der Veer, Jacob	A lot,	"	8 " "
Van Laer, Adriaen	"	New Amsterdam,	15 " "
Kip, Jacob	"	"	15 " "
Jorissen, Abram	32 morgens,	Midwout,	15 " "
Hegeman, Adriaen	59 "	"	
West, John	26 "	Mespath,	17 June, "
Elbertsen, Elbert	18 "	Amersfoort,	19 " "
Van Curler, Arent et al.	An Indian tract	Schonowe (Schenec'dy,)	27 July "
Ellis, Bastiaen	8 morgens,	Manhattans,	19 Aug. "
Bergen, town of	Township,	Pavonia,	5 Sept. "
Wandal, Thomas	4 morgens,	Mespath,	6 " "
Utrecht, town of New	Township	Long Island,	22 Dec. "
Swartwout, Cornelis	24 morgens,	Midwout,	13 Jan'y, 1662
Bronck, Pieter	126 "	Koexhacking,	13 " "
Carpesy, Gabriel	A lot,	New Amsterdam,	20 " "
Buys, Jan Cornelis	28 morgens	Midwout,	23 " "
Van Ruyven, Cornelis	32 "	"	23 " "
Lott, Pieter	32 "	"	23 " "
Polhemus, Rev. J. Th.	24 "	"	25 " "
Shrick, Paulus	2 "	The Kolck, New Amst.	31 " "
Chambers, Thomas	4-1/2 "	Pisseman's Hoek, Esopus	10 Mar. "
Van der Grist, P.L. etal.	58 "	Manhattans,	14 " "
Bout, Jan Everts	58 "	Midwout,	17 " "
Van Dickhuys, Teunis H.	17 "	"	17 " "
Schenectady,	The great flatt of	Confirmed,	6 April "
Laurensen, Arent	A lot,	New Amsterdam,	10 May "
Van Hoesen, Jan Jansen	An Indian tract,	Claverack,	5 June, "
Church of N. Amsterdam	A lot,	New Amsterdam,	7 July, "
Bonns, Jannetje	"	"	7 " "
Teunissen, Claes	5 morgens,	Manhattans	12 Oct. "
Wemp, J.B. et al.	Martin's Island,	Schenectady,	12 Nov. "
Slecht, Corns. Barents	25 morgens,	Esopus	7 Dec. "
Neilsen, Niels, Sen. et al.	Verdrietje Hoeck,	Delaware,	5 Mar. 1663
Dupuis, Nicolaes et al.	A plantation	Staten Island,	19 " "
Sluyter, Hendrick Jans	A lot,	New Amsterdam,	2 April, "
Van Schaick, G.G. et al.	33 Morgens,	A new town, Esopus,	16 " "
Schuyler, P.P.	34 "	"	20 " "
Anthony, Allard et al.	45 "	Manhattans,	25 " "
Broersen, Jan et al.	5 "	Wiltwyck,	25 " "
De Wever, Jan	21 "	Esopus	25 " "
Bronck, Pieter	A lot	Beverwyck,	
Crepel, Anthony	8 m. of Kaelcop's land	Esopus,	25 " "
Oosterhout, J. Jans	A lot,	Wiltwyck,	
Blanchan, Matys	"	"	
Wynkoop, Cornelis	12 morgens,	Esopus	25 " "

Names of Patentees.	Description of Grant.	Location of Grant.	Date of Patent.
Du Bois, Louis	20 morgens.	Esopus	25 April, 1663
Swartwout, Roeloffe	20 "	"	25 " "
Van Holsteyn, H'k Corns.	2 "	"	25 " "
Mol, Lambert Huyberts	21 "	"	25 " "
Tomassen, Jan	33 "	"	26 " "
Jans, Volckert	33 "	"	28 " "
Groot, Symon Symons	A lot,	Beverwyck	11 May "
Bancker, Gerrit	22 morgens,	Schenectady,	16 June "
Tomassen, Jan	An Island,	Schotack	3 Nov. "
Leendertsen, Albert	A lot,	New Amsterdam,	8 Dec. "
Varleth, Nicolaes	21 morgens,	Esopus	10 " "
Jacobsen, Casper	A lot,	Beverwyck,	29 " "
Slot, Jan Pietersen	8 morgens and 2 lots	Van Cuelen's hook,H'rlm	4 Jan'y, 1664
Snediker, Gerrit	34-1/2 morgens	Midwout,	24 " "
Swartwout, Cornelis	29 morgens	"	24 " "
Huybertsen, Adriaen	24 "	Mespath,	26 " "
Krygier, Capt. Martin	A lot,	New Amsterdam	26 " "
Van Ruyven, Cornelis	42 morgens,	Midwout,	26 " "
Claesen, Claes	26 "	New Utrecht,	29 " "
Meyer, Nichs.(van Holst'n)	40 "	New Haerlem,	29 " "
Tomassen, Jan	A lot,	Beverwyck,	10 Mar. "
Van Vorst, Ide Cornelis	"	Ahasimus,	5 April "
" "	"	Schreyer's Hook,N.A.	5 " "
Stoutenbergh, Pieter	4 morgens,	Manhattans,	7 " "
Pietersen, Hendrick	25 "	Midwout,	7 " "
Syboutsen, Hark	8 "	Middelburgh,	18 " "
Chambers, Thomas	26 "	Esopus,	22 " "
Loockermans, Govert	26 "	Mespath,	22 " "
Hendricksen, Gerrit	Certain meadows,	Manhattans,	3 May, "
Chambers, Marg't wf. of Thomas,	48 morgens	Esopus	12 " "
Hansen, Michel	20 "	New Bedford, Wallebout,	15 " "
Grim, Otto	A lot,	New Amsterdam,	15 " "
De Decker, Jan	60 morgens	Staten Island,	15 " "
Philips, Fredrick	A lot,	Wiltwyck,	17 " "
Trynbolt, Pieter Jans	"	New Amsterdam,	17 " "
De Witt, Jan (the miller)	"	The Kolck, N.A.	27 " "
Vinchardt, Adriaen	"	" "	1 June, "
Van Nes, Cornelis	21 morgens,	Schenectady,	16 " "
Cornelissen, Teunis	24 "	"	16 " "
De Bakker, Symon	24 "	"	16 " "
Adriaensen, Pieter	26 "	"	16 " "
Teller, Willem	23 "	"	16 " "
Schuyler, Philip P.	An Indian tract,	Halfmoon, Moh'k River,	10 July, "
Paul, Thomas et al.	"	Now, town of Stuyvesant,	10 " "
Hallet, Willem	"	Sintsinck, L.I.	1 Aug. "
Van Hooghten, Frans. J.	A lot,	New Amsterdam,	3 " "
Rvcken, Abram	Hullett's Island,	Near Hellegat,	19 " "
Bavard, Petrus	130 morgens	Esopus,	19 " "
Roose, Albert Heymans	A plantation	"	19 " "

N.B. A morgen is a Dutch land measure, equal to about two acres.

A TABLE OF STATISTICS ON DUTCH IMMIGRATION TO AMERICA

Period	No. of Dutch-born admitted to U. S.
1841–1855	13,195
1856–1860	3,806
1861–1865	2,149
1866–1870	7,129
1871–1875	10,394
1876–1880	6,147
1881–1885	20,350
1886–1890	23,451
1891–1895	20,754
1896–1900	6,004
1901–1905	18,501
1906–1910	29,761
1911–1915	31,392
1916–1920	12,374

Total officially admitted: 205,407 between 1841 and 1920

Year	No. of Dutch-born residents of U. S.	
1900	105,000	(of which 30,000 in Mich., 22,000 in Illinois)
1910	135,000	
1920	131,766	(of which 33,499 in Mich., 14,344 in Ill.)
1930	133,133	(of which 32,128 still in Mich., mainly in Grand Rapids, Kalamazoo and Holland)
1960	118,415	(large concentrations in California, as well as traditional areas)

111

BIBLIOGRAPHICAL AIDS

A SELECTIVE ANNOTATED BIBLIOGRAPHY OF WORKS ABOUT THE DUTCH IN AMERICA

John Romeyn Brodhead (compiler) and E. B. O'Callaghan (editor), <u>Documents Relative to the Colonial History of the State of New York.</u> Volume I. New York, 1856.

The first volume of this massive collection includes documents relating to the period of Dutch rule, such as land grants, correspondence about the Indian Wars, peace treaties with the Indians, and decrees of the West India Company. All the Dutch material has been translated into English.

Henry S. Lucas, <u>Netherlanders in America: Dutch Immigration to the United States and Canada, 1789-1950.</u> 744 p.

This is an exhaustive treatment of the nineteenth century Dutch settlements in the midwest and their founders. Lucas includes chapters on the church, education and the press, as well as extensive notes and an appendix containing immigration and church membership statistics. There is a useful index of names.

---------------Dutch Immigrant Memoirs and Related Writings. Assen, 1955. 2 volumes.

A fascinating collection for the student of Dutch midwestern settlements and their early days. Lucas has translated the Dutch entries, of which he also includes the original. There is an index.

E. B. O'Callaghan, <u>History of New Netherland, or, New York under the Dutch.</u> New York, 1848. 2 volumes.,

This is an exhaustive chronicle based upon Dutch colonial annals. The appendix is valuable, containing documents from the period pertaining to the West India Company and to patroonships, as well as an interesting list of the names of the people to whom land grants were made by the Company. There is an index.

J. Van Hinte, <u>Nederlanders in Amerika.</u> Groningen, 1928. 2 volumes.

Since Van Hinte's work is in Dutch, it remains of limited use to an American audience. We have included it here because not only is it the first and the most detailed of the general works, but because it has pictures, maps, and an extensive bibliography of books and pamphlets, many of which are in English, which would be of interest to the American reader who commands no Dutch.

Bertus Harry Wabeke, <u>Dutch Emigration to America 1624-1860.</u> New York, 1944. 160 p.

Wabeke gives a very readable and accurate short account of the colonial period, with maps and pictures; there are also two chapters on the "New Immigration" of the nineteenth century. There is a long bibliography of relevant books and pamphlets.

Van de Luyster, Jannes, 18
Van den Bosch, Koene, 19, 27
Van den Broek, Theodorus, 19, 21, 27
Van den Heuvel, Gerhard, 21, 27
Vanderbilt, Cornelius, 11
Van der Casteele, Eduard, 30
Van der Donck, Adriaen, 4, 5
Van der Kemp, Francois, 11, 13
Van der Meulen, Cornelius, 18
Van der Wall, Giles, 29
Van der Werp, Douwe, 29
Van Lieuwen, John, 36
Van Noppen, Leonard, 34
Van Peyma, Worp, 23
Van Raalte, Albertus, 15, 16, 17, 18, 19, 25, 27, 29
Van Rensselaer, Jan, 4

Van Rensselaer, Kiliaen, 2, 4
Van Tongeren, Jan, 19
Van Twiller, Wouter, 1
Van Velzen, Simon, 15
Verboort, John, 26
Verhulst, Willem, 1
Verplanck, Gulian, 12
Vorst, C., 29

Welling, A. M., 26
Wilhelmina, Queen, 32
William I, King, 15
Wormser, Andreas, 25
Wyckoff, Isaac, 17

Ypma, Maarten, 18

Zonne, Pieter, 21